Date: 7/22/22

PA░ S0-BZO-174
LIBRARY SYSTEM

3650 Summit Boulevard
West Palm Beach, FL 33406

My Next Life as a VILLAINESS: ALL ROUTES LEAD TO DOOM!

VOLUME 4

SATORU YAMAGUCHI
ILLUSTRATIONS BY NAMI HIDAKA

My Next Life as a Villainess: All Routes Lead to Doom! Volume 4
by Satoru Yamaguchi

Translated by Shirley Yeung
Edited by Aimee Zink
Layout by Leah Waig
English Front Cover by Carl Vanstiphout
English Spine + Back Cover Design by Kelsey Denton
Manga Lettering by Kimberly Pham

This book is a work of fiction. Names, characters, places, and incidents are the product of the author's imagination or are used fictitiously. Any resemblance to actual events, locales, or persons, living or dead, is coincidental.

Copyright © 2016 Satoru Yamaguchi
Illustrations by Nami Hidaka

First published in Japan in 2016 by Ichijinsha Inc., Tokyo.
Publication rights for this English edition arranged through Kodansha Ltd., Tokyo.

All rights reserved. In accordance with the U.S. Copyright Act of 1976, the scanning, uploading, and electronic sharing of any part of this book without the permission of the publisher is unlawful piracy and theft of the author's intellectual property.

Find more books like this one at www.j-novel.club!

President and Publisher: Samuel Pinansky
Managing Editor (Novels): Aimee Zink
QA Manager: Hannah N. Carter
Marketing Manager: Stephanie Hii

ISBN: 978-1-7183-6663-3
Printed in Korea
First Printing: November 2020
10 9 8 7 6 5 4 3 2 1

Contents

My Next Life as a Villainess:

Jeord Stuart

Third prince of the kingdom, and Katarina's fiancé. Although he looks like a fairy-tale prince with his blonde hair and blue eyes, he secretly harbors a twisted and terrible nature. He once spent his days in boredom, never showing interest in anything, until he met Katarina Claes. His magical element is Fire.

Larna Smith
A very talented woman who holds a high position in the Magical Ministry.

Sora
A young man wielding the Dark Arts, in service to the Ministry. Fond of Katarina.

Raphael Wolt
A young man working at the Magical Ministry. A calm and capable person.

Alexander
A magical tool created by Larna. Physically appears to be a bear-shaped plush toy.

Jeffrey Stuart
The first prince of the kingdom. Most people see him as flippant because of his always-smiling, relaxed demeanor.

Katarina Claes

The only daughter of Duke Claes. Has slanted eyes and angled features, which she thinks make her look like a villainess. After memories of her past life returned, she transformed from a spoiled noble lady to a problem child. Although she often gets ahead of herself, she is honest and straightforward. She has below-average academic and magical ability. Her magical element is Earth.

Susanna Randall
The second daughter of Marquess Randall. The first prince's fiancée.

Luigi Claes
Katarina's father, a Duke and the head of the Claes family who spoils his daughter.

All Routes Lead to Doom!

Nicol Ascart

The son of Royal Chancellor Ascart. An incredibly beautiful and alluring young man who loves his sister, Sophia, deeply. His magical element is Wind.

Keith Claes

Katarina's adopted brother, taken in by the Claes family due to his magical aptitude. Considerably handsome, and seen by others as a chivalrous ladies' man. His magical element is Earth.

Alan Stuart

Jeord's twin brother, and the fourth prince of the kingdom. Wildly handsome but also surly and arrogant. Often compares himself to his genius brother, and sulks when he realizes he can't catch up. His magical element is Water.

Sophia Ascart

Daughter of Royal Chancellor Ascart, and Nicol's younger sister. Used to face discrimination due to her white hair and red eyes. A calm and peaceful girl.

Maria Campbell

A commoner, but also a rare "Wielder of Light." The original protagonist of *Fortune Lover* who is very hardworking and loves baking.

Mary Hunt

Fourth daughter of Marquess Hunt, and Alan's fiancée. A lovely and charming girl who's well known as the perfect image of a noble lady.

Milidiana Claes

Katarina's mother, and wife of Duke Claes. Has very angled features like her daughter.

Anne Shelley

Katarina's personal maid who has been with her since childhod.

Noticing that it was now somewhat later in the afternoon, I hastened my footsteps. Surely they would be worried about me if I took too long. I hurried through the street that had just been bustling with activity only a while ago. It was now sparse, quiet — it was, after all, time for dinner. Delicious smells wafted from the commoners' homes as I walked by.

I adjusted my grip on the bag that held a variety of sweets, the kind that were only sold to commoners in the downtown districts. It had been a while since we'd had anything like this, so I knew she would be happy. As I thought about the person who would be most pleased by these candies upon my return, a smile naturally formed on my face.

I had come to purchase them in secret. Under normal circumstances, I would have never set out suddenly to do anything like what I was doing now. But she had been through a lot lately, and I thought that this would make her happy. That was why I'd come here.

However, the shops were busier than I thought, and the whole endeavor took longer than expected. I started walking even faster, making my way through the streets under the now-orange sky. That was when it happened.

Someone was now standing before me. If I had to guess, they most likely stepped out from one of the countless alleyways and side roads that branched off this one. A deep hood and cloak covered their form, but the individual did not look very bulky. In fact, I could see a bit of a dress underneath that cape…

A woman, perhaps? Who could this be? It was strange that they would just appear right there and then, so coincidentally, as if to bump into me. No… this person was standing there intentionally. In fact, they were now staring at me in a most suspicious manner.

"It's been a while," the person before me said. A woman's voice, unmistakably. However… it was not a voice I recognized.

"…And who might you be?" I asked in a low voice, alarmed.

The woman responded in an almost theatrical way as she slowly closed the distance between us. "Ahh, you really shouldn't say that, you know? Asking who I am… as if we were complete strangers," the woman said, pulling her hood down. Her long hair cascaded down her back.

"Ah!" Shocked and bewildered, I stared at the woman.

The woman merely smiled, the corners of her carmine-red lips curling up. "Say… there is a certain wish I would like fulfilled. You'll hear me out, won't you?"

Upon hearing the woman's needlessly dramatic voice, I felt my expression stiffen. The look on my face right now would most likely be described as grave.

"That's quite enough! Please wake up this instant, young miss. If you continue to dally, you will be late for your lessons!"

I could hear a voice that was getting increasingly strict. I opened my heavy eyelids reluctantly. The curtains had been drawn back, and the sun's rays were streaming in.

With a mighty yawn, I stretched, rubbing my half-closed eyes absent-mindedly. As soon as I got up, Anne, my personal maid, immediately started doing my hair and getting me ready for the day. After thanking her for her efforts, I finally got up from the bed, still half-asleep. It was time to get ready and set off for campus.

It had been almost two years since I, Katarina Claes, started attending the Academy of Magic. It was such a short time ago, but I was already close to graduation. *Ah... how time flies.*

Now that I thought about it, when I first came here, I wasn't even sure I'd make it to graduation safely. Things turned out very differently than I'd expected. I thought back on how things had been back then as I remembered last year's opening ceremony.

I am the daughter of Duke Claes. I am indeed a noble lady, and I suppose there aren't too many daughters of dukes hanging around in this kingdom. But despite my relatively high social standing, I am still very much a normal girl on the inside.

If there's one abnormal thing about me, it would be the fact that I tripped and hit my head on a rock when I was eight, and the impact caused me to remember all the memories of my previous life.

My previous life... I was born to a normal salaryman, and was the oldest daughter of the family. I eventually grew into an upstanding otaku high-school girl. I spent my day absorbed in manga, anime, and games, and it was wonderful. Those days wouldn't last, though; I ended up dying due to an unfortunate accident.

After that, I was reincarnated as Duke Claes' daughter. Of all the people to be reborn as, I found myself in the shoes of Katarina Claes, villainess extraordinaire! She was the antagonist of *Fortune Lover,* the otome game I was playing before my untimely death.

Fortune Lover was highly recommended by an otaku friend of mine. Katarina was the main villain of this game, the fiancée of one of the romanceable characters, and also the protagonist's rival. Yes, that's right — I had been reincarnated as one of the most annoying characters in that game I had been playing...

9

To make things worse, there were no good endings for Katarina! She was a villainess who only had bad ends… being exiled from the kingdom if the protagonist got a happy ending, or getting killed if she got a bad one. There was no winning with this character.

This was the truth that I realized at the age of eight. This was why I had worked hard, coming up with various countermeasures to subvert the game's Catastrophic Bad Ends. I simply had to prepare as much as I could before the game started — at the opening ceremony of the Academy of Magic.

I kept this one goal in mind, my determination that I would not lose to any of these Catastrophic Bad Ends, as I started attending the Academy of Magic in the spring of last year. To think that it would all end uneventfully in the form of the Friendship Ending, of all things…

The game's protagonist, Maria, was beautiful, gentle, and was very good at baking. She would be the first person on anyone's mind if they were looking for a bride. She was a very charming girl. But when the game's timeline finally ended during last year's graduation ceremony, I was greeted with an unexpected reality — everyone stayed friends, and with that Friendship Ending, I made it through the end of the graduation ceremony without any problems.

It was a surprising and sudden end to things. As a result, I didn't end up using a single one of the countermeasures I'd prepared. The Catastrophic Bad Ends passed me by, and just like that, they were all gone. I safely advanced into my second year at the academy.

While I did get into some trouble after that, things eventually worked out, and it would be time to graduate soon. These recent days had been peaceful, almost unbelievably so, considering how I felt when I first came to the academy.

We had fewer lessons now that we were approaching the end of the year, though I did have some classes today. Even my grades, which were pretty shaky in the beginning, were now somewhat more stable thanks to my skilled friends.

All that time I had spent worrying about exile or losing my life to the game's machinations seemed far away in the past now, almost as if those problems never existed to begin with. But as I approached my graduation, I was now suddenly faced with a new problem...

"Young miss, flowers and a letter for you have arrived again," Anne said, handing the items over.

The bouquet was cute, with pinkish flowers at its base. But when I saw it, I let out a sigh. These bouquets were the one problem I found myself faced with these days, now that I had overcome all the Catastrophic Bad Ends.

"We're going to see each other again soon, right? He doesn't need to keep sending these flowers and stuff..."

Anne laughed wryly as she neatly transferred the flowers into a vase. Though it wasn't every single day, the flowers were showing up on a regular basis, which was clear from the fact that my room was filled with them.

Picking up the letter that arrived with the bouquet, I sighed, audibly louder than I had before. I supposed the letter contained more prose and poetry to make me blush — after all, I had zero experience when it came to things like love.

...*Why did Jeord get like this all of a sudden?* The one who had sent me this letter, and all these bouquets, was none other than Jeord Stuart.

Jeord Stuart was originally one of the potential love interests in the world of *Fortune Lover*. He was the third prince, and a genius at just about everything. As a result, he grew tired of this world, and lived each and every day in boredom. Upon enrolling into the Academy of Magic, however, Jeord would cross paths with the bright, lovable, and innocently simple protagonist, and then fall for her. At least, that's how the story goes.

Of course, the antagonist would show up to get in the way of the protagonist's love. Said antagonist was me, Katarina Claes. In the story of *Fortune Lover,* Katarina sustained an injury to her forehead while playing with Jeord when she was younger. Using this as an excuse, she pressured Jeord into an engagement. Upon noticing that Jeord had feelings for the protagonist, Katarina would then do everything she could to get in their way — including bullying and sabotage.

As a result, she would eventually be tried for her sins and exiled from the kingdom... or she would rush at the protagonist with a blade, only to be cut down by Jeord and die. Yes, Katarina only ever had Catastrophic Bad Ends.

Honestly, though, I didn't do anything like that to Maria. In fact, I ended up utterly terrifying and scaring away those who had been attempting to bully my cute and wonderful friend. And I hadn't latched onto Jeord at all! I even requested multiple times for the engagement to be called off!

Even so, should an unexpected Catastrophic Bad End come for me one day, I had made my preparations. To be exact, I had set aside a complete set of agricultural tools for me to escape with if I were exiled from the kingdom. And then there were the projectile snake toys that I had made...

Although no one got in their way, Maria and Jeord never did get an ending of any kind. And in the end, I was unable to get Jeord to cancel our engagement — and so I still remained his fiancée even as I advanced into my second year at the academy.

From what I knew of *Fortune Lover*'s plot, Jeord had only kept Katarina in the engagement as a means of deflecting other potentially interested suitors. That was why I'd expected Jeord to fall for some other woman instead of Maria… and if that happened, my role would be over. I never doubted that. In fact, I was simply hoping for Jeord to find a partner soon! Those were my usual thoughts on the matter.

But… something completely unexpected happened recently. It was during the school festival. I had been on cloud nine from the fact that I had safely overcome the Catastrophic Bad Ends. I was even thinking of enjoying myself to the fullest during the famed school festival at the academy. But then I found myself in trouble again when I was suddenly kidnapped.

While I did get kidnapped, nothing terrible was done to me. Perhaps I had been riding a little bit too confidently on the coattails of my recent success, but I had absolutely no sense of any impending danger. From what I was told, I was put to sleep with some kind of drug. When I woke up, I found myself in a room with a gentle and capable maid. I was provided with three full meals, and allowed to sleep in for however long I wanted. It was an awesome experience.

…This isn't something I'd say to my friends and everyone else, of course, since they'd been so worried about me, but it felt a lot easier to live in that room than in my quarters back at the dorm or at Claes Manor.

Although I was enjoying myself, kidnapping was a crime, and soon enough, my friends rescued me from the manor where I was being held captive. It was then that it happened — Jeord kissed me.

It was the first kiss I'd ever experienced in my life. Well, if I were to count my previous life, it would be the first one in two lifetimes! It was too sudden, and I soon passed out from the confusion.

When I woke up the next day, the only conclusion I could draw was that it was all a dream. After all, I was nothing more than a deterrent to Jeord, meant to fend off other suitors. At least, that was what I thought, so... why?

When I crossed paths with Jeord back at the academy again, he had the sweetest expression I had ever seen on his face, and he leaned in for yet another kiss.

"So you thought it was a dream? But I assure you... what happened just now, and what happened then — neither of those were dreams," he'd said, smiling faintly.

"B-But why?"

I was still shaken by the events when Jeord hit me with the stunning truth.

"I presume you are asking about the kiss, yes? But of course, Katarina, it is because I love you so."

It was unbelievable. Stunning. Shocking, really. To think the day would come that I, someone who was never destined to have love in my life, would be confessed to... And on top of all that, by a potential love interest in an otome game, too! A fairy-tale prince!

When Jeord was just a two-dimensional image on a screen, he always looked lovingly at the player. But for an actual three-dimensional Jeord to be looking at me in such a way, right in front of my face! *Wah!* I could feel my face heating up as I re-lived the memory.

Ugh... what should I do? If I were the popular protagonist of an otome game, then maybe I would be better equipped to deal with a proposal or two, no matter how many suitors approached me. But... I was nothing more than an innocent girl in my previous life — one who never even had the slightest brush with love. Yes, I had zero experience points in the love category.

I was just proposed to for the first time in this, and my previous, lifetimes! All I could do was remain shaken, panicking and bumbling this way and that. To make things worse, the person proposing to me was a popular and handsome prince! I could feel the mental tremors increasing in intensity.

"Ahh…" Once again, I let a long, drawn-out sigh escape from my lips.

"But… why me, of all people?"

"Huh? What are you going on about suddenly, Big Sister?"

I was muttering continuously as I finished my preparations and started heading toward the academy. Before leaving, Keith, my kind and gentle adopted brother, would always meet up with me so that we could walk to class together.

"It's about Prince Jeord… I don't understand why it would be me…"

"Ah, that. I see," Keith said, sounding lonely. The expression on his face was stiff, which was enough for me to know that Keith was different from his usual self.

"I mean, Prince Jeord… he's so popular, right? So many girls would love to marry him."

It was true, Prince Jeord was very popular amongst the ladies of the kingdom. Not only was he a handsome prince, he was also intelligent, and capable at sports. To top it all off, his magical capabilities were impressive too. It was simply impossible for a lady to not be entranced with this seemingly perfect man. As a result, Jeord had been approached by many noble ladies, even with Katarina Claes as his fiancée.

"Surely he has many wonderful candidates to choose from?" I continued. After all, it was that way in the game too. Jeord lived his days in boredom and relative disinterest until he crossed paths with the bright and innocent protagonist, and fell for her in the process. "In that case, why would he choose someone like me? Someone so… unremarkable?"

While I was the daughter of a duke, I was born with the face of a villainess — I was hardly stunning or beautiful in the traditional sense. I wasn't smart, either, and my magical power was dismally weak. I was terrible at dancing too, and the only things I was good at were climbing trees and catching fish. Really… I was just a normal girl.

"What does Prince Jeord see in my normal, uninteresting, and plain self…?" I really couldn't wrap my head around it.

"Big Sister… perhaps it would do you well to look up the definition of 'normal' in a dictionary," my adopted brother responded with a faraway look in his eyes.

"Hm?" *What's that supposed to mean?* I could almost feel a question mark floating above my head.

"Good morning, Katarina," a breezy voice called out from behind me.

Ah, speak of the devil… I turned around, and as expected, the person in question was approaching me with a brilliant smile on his face. Katarina Claes' fiancé, and the third prince of the kingdom… Jeord Stuart.

"…Good morning. Prince Jeord," I responded, still somewhat shaken.

Jeord wasted no time in closing the distance between us. "I have sent flowers and a letter today. Did you receive them safely, pray tell?" he said, now at incredibly close range.

T-Too close! Far too close! The presence of this three-dimensional beautiful human being will be the end of my poor heart! Although

I had simply dismissed this kind of thing before, thinking that perhaps Prince Jeord was simply bad at gauging normal distance between people, I had grown used to it and accepted it as a way of life. But lately I couldn't dismiss it like I had before.

"U-Um... Prince Jeord, you're a little..." *Too close. Could you please step away a little?* was what I would have liked to say... but Jeord had retreated before I had finished my sentence.

Now that I took a good look though, I saw that it wasn't Jeord stepping back on his own volition — he had been pulled back by the hand of someone else. "Prince Jeord. You are a little too close, are you not?"

The one who had pulled Jeord away was Keith. He had a remarkable smile on his face too, one that was comparable to Jeord's. *Ah, thank you, my dear brother. Thanks to you, the integrity of my heart and its chambers has been preserved... for now.*

"Keith. Katarina and I will be united in marriage one day. I do not see the issue with me being a little closer with her," said Jeord as he extended his arm and placed a hand on my cheek. I involuntarily shivered at the sensation of his fingertips brushing across my face, and quickly retreated to a safe distance.

Keith, upon seeing this, furrowed his brow. "What marriage? You are scaring her, do you not see? Please, this way, Big Sister..."

I quickly hid behind Keith's back, grateful for his quick thinking. *But dear brother of mine... I would not exactly say that I was scared...*

"Ah... but you see, Katarina is not scared of me — hardly! She is merely becoming aware of my presence."

It was as if Jeord was reading my mind! What he said was true. I wasn't scared of him, no... but I wasn't used to these things, especially when it came to love, so I was caught off guard. *As expected of the perfect Prince Jeord… he really does see through everything.* I couldn't help but feel a sense of appreciation for Jeord's sharp senses, even as I continued hiding behind Keith.

"Unlike a certain someone, who does not seem to register in her mind in the slightest… no, not even a fragment," Jeord said with that same defiant smile.

I felt Keith twitch at those words. *Register? Mind? Hmm? Who is Jeord talking about? Judging by the way Keith reacted… Does he know who it is?*

Looking up at Keith, I was surprised to see a certain sorrow in his features. "Um…" Just as I was about to call out to him—

"Good morning, Lady Katarina." That cheerful greeting was from Mary Hunt, a close friend of mine. She was here with her fiancé, Alan Stuart. Her bright voice immediately dispelled the strange atmosphere that had been hanging over us.

"Good morning, Mary, Prince Alan." I returned her greeting with a smile. Mary responded in kind. *Ah, her smile really is lovely.*

Mary was the very image of a noble lady. She had that perfect smile and aura of elegance no matter the occasion, whether at an event in noble circles or a public space. The smile she showed when speaking to us was different, though. It was warmer.

On the other hand, Alan, who had been trailing behind Mary, simply responded with a simple "Yeah." There wasn't much to his greeting, but this was how he always was. He was nowhere near as friendly as Jeord. Maybe he could just use a tiny bit more of Jeord's sociability, but Alan's fans actually preferred his gruff nature.

I was baffled by this whole situation. The complexities of a maiden's heart were indeed numerous. With the two of them here, the atmosphere changed. Mary, who had been smiling at me just a second ago, now suddenly had the smile she usually reserved for social affairs on her face.

"Well, if it isn't Prince Jeord. Is it really alright for you to be here at this point in time? I do recall quite the amount of work piling up at the council chambers…" she said to Jeord. While it almost seemed like Mary was actually worried about unfinished work at the council, that strange atmosphere was back again.

"Why yes, it was quite the workload indeed. However, all I had to do was put my mind to it. I have already finished it all, you see."

"I see… how nice to hear…"

Hmm. What is this? It's Mary's smile, sure, but something about it seems off.

"Even so," Jeord continued, "I feel like the workload at the council has increased quite a bit as of late. I wonder why that would be the case?"

"Perhaps it is due to the impending graduation ceremony?"

"Is that so? It almost feels as if a certain individual is funneling work toward me, so as to unjustly rob me of my time… I cannot help but think of that, no?"

"Surely you jest, Prince Jeord. Perhaps your work and tiredness have gotten the better of you, for you to become delusional like that? Perhaps it would be best for you to get some quality rest on your own today?"

"Hmm. Perhaps I shall simply attribute it to that for now. However, no matter how much work gets piled up on my desk, I will hardly see it as a trial of any kind."

"Ahaha. As expected of you, Prince Jeord. I see you are as capable as ever."

Although the two were all smiles, the aura emanating from their conversation was somewhat unpleasant.

"Good morning, everyone. Should we not be headed to the campus soon? We will be late if we dally…" a somewhat sleepy, yet panicked Sophia said.

With that, the conversation ended, and we all headed toward our classrooms together.

By the way, it seemed that Sophia did oversleep, as I'd thought. Apparently she'd stayed up all night reading novels again. The one she was reading sounded really good, so I asked to borrow it from her.

When we finally reached campus, we waited for Maria, who lived in a different dormitory. Then we all went to our classrooms to attend the few remaining lectures this term.

"I went to the Ministry yesterday and met with Lady Larna. She was eager for you to come along next time as well, Lady Katarina," Maria told me when our lecture ended and lunch break began.

Maria Campbell: the original protagonist of the otome game, *Fortune Lover,* and one of the few Wielders of Light in the kingdom. Maria had decided to work for the Ministry after her graduation. With our lessons at the academy steadily decreasing in frequency, Maria had been visiting the Ministry.

Maria's future superior was Larna Smith, someone I had met during a certain incident not long ago. I didn't know who she was then, but I'd spent some time with her when she was going by "Lana." She was easy to talk to, and seemed like a candid person who didn't mince her words. I never would have guessed that she was actually some important person from the Ministry!

From what I'd heard, Larna had a senior position, too. For some reason she'd become interested in me, and arrangements were made for me to start working at the Ministry after I graduated. In fact, she was personally recommending me for the position.

If I were to just graduate normally, it was likely that Jeord would whisk me away to formally become his bride. I mean, it's not like I disliked him. But the problem was that he was royalty, and if I married him, I'd become royalty too! Honestly, maintaining my social status as the daughter of a duke already took too much effort. Even if I tried my best to play the role, Mother always complained about my performance.

It hadn't taken me long after regaining my memories to realize that I wasn't cut out for this noble thing at all. I'd make a better farmer, or at least some common townsperson. But me, of all people, becoming royalty? Standing at the top of the kingdom...?

A little while ago, I was pondering what I'd do with my life once Jeord found someone he really liked and called off his engagement with me. Most nobles preferred that their daughters get married as soon as possible, but my family was different. My father spoiled me like crazy, and my mother couldn't care less. *"Let Katarina do as she pleases!"* my father said. My mother replied, *"If she were to get married, she'd embarrass herself even further. Wouldn't it be better for her to stay home instead?"* So the two of them never really campaigned for me to get married.

This was why I had been happily thinking about what I could do after graduation without a care in the world, only for Jeord to suddenly go on an all-out romantic offensive. At this rate, I'd really end up becoming a member of the royal family!

To prevent that, I had to enter the ranks of the Ministry at all costs. The one who had informed me of this potential way out was Raphael, a friend of mine who was currently working at the Ministry. After all, the Ministry was the next most powerful organization in the kingdom, second to royalty. So joining the Ministry's ranks would provide me with some protection. Even if a prince wanted to marry me, I couldn't simply be whisked away to the royal castle.

Although that was supposed to be my salvation, and the only way out of this mess… I now wasn't so sure. After all, my magical power was low — the bottom of the barrel at the academy, really. If I was good at my studies then maybe I could join the Ministry as a researcher or academic, but my grades were average at best.

Would a normal, relatively boring and plain girl like myself have any business tunneling into the Ministry, the nest of elites? Although I was often scolded by my parents in my past life for being brazen and cheeky, this was too much for me. I didn't have any skills or abilities, and to just wiggle my way into the most elite organization in the kingdom via a connection… it felt wrong, even for me.

So I hadn't given Larna a response yet, even after she went out of her way to invite me into the Ministry. Of course, I didn't expect to suddenly have powers on par with Maria's, but I at least wanted one special skill of some kind that would mean I could enter the Ministry without shame.

All I could do was keep trying to come up with something, all while giving Maria vague answers, despite her earnest push for me to join the Ministry with her. There were only a few months left until graduation, and the path I would take remained undecided.

Ever since his proposal after the kidnapping incident, Jeord's aggressively romantic approaches showed no signs of stopping. With his beautiful face, Jeord would approach me elegantly, then lean in with whispers of love and desire for intimacy. These incidents turned me various shades of pale blue and deep red, and my friends would come to my rescue each time.

But honestly, I had zero resistance when it came to love, and I felt like my poor heart couldn't possibly keep up. I felt like my heartbeats in this short span of time had already gone way past the heartbeat count of the rest of my lifespan combined.

Honestly, having a handsome prince like this almost tackle me with his aggressive approaches was… difficult. For a novice at love like me, shouldn't we start with exchanging notes or something like that instead?! I'd prefer a slower start like that!

Today was the same as ever. Jeord's relentless approaches had left me tired, and I now found myself in Keith's quarters. "I'm… s-so tired," I groaned. With that, I collapsed on Keith's sofa, taking up the whole thing myself and complaining all the while.

Keith, however, merely smiled bitterly at my antics. "Ready to give up, I see," he said, while handing me some snacks I liked and pouring the tea I loved.

"Fan kyuu…" I said, with my mouth stuffed full of the snacks he'd offered me. Normally, Keith would be upset at my lack of manners. But today, he merely looked on with that smile and forgave my transgressions.

I'd been doing this for a few days — sneaking into Keith's room and doing nothing but complaining the entire time. But he never once seemed bothered by it, and instead listened with an empathetic ear. I really did have a wonderful brother.

Come to think of it, Keith had always been covering my tracks and supporting me ever since we were children. He was always there after I was lectured by Mother, or if I messed up at a tea-party. He would stay with me until I cheered up.

It made me think of my boisterous big brother in my past life. Upon seeing his sister depressed, he would usually cheer me up, although he chose to do it with a pro-wrestling move. That was the kind of brother he was. I didn't dislike him or anything, but I always found myself thinking, *Maybe you should understand the intricacies of a maiden's heart, or at least try, you dummy!*

Compared to him, Keith had a much better understanding of those intricacies. Even if he did get something wrong, he would never come at me with some pro-wrestling move. Instead, he'd present me with snacks and tea that I liked. Keith was gentle, caring, and considerate — he really was a wonderful brother. He would never have any issues marrying into any other noble family. Well, I suppose our family would be the one the bride would be getting married into, not the other way around.

Keith would definitely be very popular amongst the ladies. As his adoptive older sister, I really did hope that Keith would find a good bride. At the very least, not someone like Mother... that would be really worrisome. The ideal was someone like Maria, cute and kind.

Just as I was indulging myself in the thoughts of who my adoptive younger brother should marry...

"Hey, Big Sister... do you really have reservations about marrying Prince Jeord?" Keith asked with a serious expression on his face.

"Of course I do, Keith! After all, if I were to marry Prince Jeord, I'd become royalty! Royalty! I'd stand at the top of this kingdom! I couldn't possibly fulfill such a role!"

Even Mary, who was the very epitome of what a noble lady should be, didn't find the prospects of becoming royalty very pleasant at all. She often talked about how troublesome it'd be. If Mary couldn't do it, there was no way I would be able to. Such was my spirited response.

"Haha. I suppose so. It would be a little difficult for you to play the role of a royal." Keith smiled, now strangely happier than before. However, his serious expression soon returned. "But... Big Sister, if you ever... feel that way about Prince Jeord..."

"Hm?"

"No. It's nothing." Keith stopped speaking. He looked sad for some reason, like how he looked way back then when he had just arrived at Claes Manor. My heart tightened at the sight.

However, Keith soon returned to his usual self and started speaking again. The conversation soon shifted to me complaining once more, and before long, I had all but forgotten about the tightness in my heart. It wasn't long before I felt refreshed and returned to my room.

We would be on a short break from the academy starting tomorrow, and I had decided to return to Claes Manor. At the very least, I would be able to escape from Jeord's intense approaches for a while. That was a relieving thought.

The next day, Keith and I returned to Claes Manor as planned. I immediately changed into my gardening overalls, and for the first time in a long time, headed into the gardens to tend to the fields.

In the past, Mother would always try to get me away from doing field work. Now, she simply said this with a tired expression: "Just... refrain from uttering those strange sounds of yours, and... do as you like, Katarina."

"I understand!" I cheerfully replied, although I wasn't quite sure what the strange sounds she was talking about were. *Have I been making strange sounds without noticing? Maybe a "haa..." here, or a "hyaah!" there...? Hmm. I guess I should be careful.*

With that, I took my hoe into my hands and... "And a one! Hup! And a two! Hup!" I started my agricultural work as usual.

As expected, Jeord didn't show up at the manor today. I supposed he was taking his rest too. And Keith immediately left after we got to the manor, claiming that he had "matters to attend to." As a result, I spent my time with Grandpa Tom and Anne, and worked hard in the fields.

In the past, Anne would make a face and say something like *"A noble lady working the fields...!"* But maybe because Anne had stuck with me every time I did field work, she now assisted me instead — if anything, she'd become more knowledgeable about agriculture than me.

She even gave me advice now! *"Ah, young miss, it is still a little too early to harvest those. Perhaps that row over there would be a better choice,"* she would say. She'd also become very skilled at planting seeds and saplings, and gave me all sorts of information. She'd suggest different fertilizers and farming tools. It was really very useful.

It had been a long time since I'd had the opportunity to do anything like this, and I was soon fully absorbed in the process. Before I knew it, the sun was already setting. It was well worth the work, though — the fields were now a lot cleaner, and we had a fair harvest of vegetables and crops.

I eagerly wished to show off the fruits of my labor, and so I found myself walking to Keith's room while still dressed in my gardening getup.

"Hey, Keith! We have made some improvements to the fields, would you like to... hmm?" I had knocked hard on the door, and it had swung open. "Huh? Has Keith not returned yet?" There was no one there — the room was empty.

Keith had left early, so I'd thought that he would have already come home by now. Was he somewhere else in the manor? I quickly located Sebastian (not really his name), our butler, and asked. He told me that Keith had not returned.

Is he out doing something that takes a lot of time? That's a bummer, but I guess there's no helping it. I turned around to return to the fields, only to cross paths with Mother, who had just left the tea room. As her eyes met mine, her demeanor changed. She was so happily speaking with the maids not long ago, but now her brow furrowed and rage flashed in her eyes.

Wh-Wha?! Why? What happened? Just because I crossed paths with her? I found myself paralyzed by Mother's piercing gaze. Her eyes shifted to look behind me, and her angry expression intensified.

Huh? What? I turned around, only to see that I had left a trail of mud and soil where I'd walked. To make things worse, this mud trail extended all the way into the corridor and back. I, of course, was still dressed in my gardening overalls... my muddy, dirty, field work gear.

This... was bad. I could instinctively feel it — a sense of primal danger. I had to escape from this place, but alas, my opponent was faster than I was. Before I could make a run for it, Mother had me by the collar.

"Katarina... you would do well to come with me... to my room..." Her voice was terrifying and low, as if she had become an emissary from hell itself.

And so I brushed off what remaining soil there was on my overalls, and was dragged to Mother's room like an unwilling prisoner. I would then be lectured for several long, tedious hours...

With the lecture finally over, I was released, and I once again found myself heading to Keith's room so that I could complain and report the results of my harvest. The sun had already set, after all. Surely he'd be in his room by now?

"Keith...?" There was no response. The room was as silent and still as it had been before.

That day, Keith didn't come home to Claes Manor.

Until now, Keith had never left home like this. Everyone was shaken. Then, just as there was talk of sending out a search party, a single letter arrived at the manor. Written in the letter was...

The pressure of carrying on the good name of Duke Claes has become too much for me. That is why I have left. Please do not search for me.
   Sincerely,
   Keith

It was written in Keith's handwriting, without a doubt. Upon receiving the letter, the entire house was thrown into chaos.

"To think that our perfect Master Keith would suddenly say that he cannot bear the pressure of succeeding the Claes name... It doesn't seem plausible."

"Did he not shadow Duke Claes on numerous occasions? Master Keith is so smart — they've been entrusting him with more important tasks recently too."

"He really did not seem to be having any problem with the pressure..."

All the servants and other staff members who worked at the manor had similar things to say. And I felt the same way. It had been over a decade since the Claes family took him in, and Keith was always capable and quick to learn. He blended into noble society very quickly, and had always been more socially agile and wittier than me. In fact, Keith was seen as the perfect heir to the Claes name. Why would he think that the pressures of inheriting that name would be overbearing?

As I sat in my room, with nearly visible question marks hovering over my head, a voice called out to me. It was my mother. *What is it? Did we get new information about Keith?*

29

"Katarina… it's about Keith," Mother said with a serious expression as she entered my room.

As I thought, she must have gotten new information. I listened intently with an equally serious expression.

"About Keith's letter… as I suspected, his disappearance does not seem related to the pressures of taking on the Claes name."

"…Of course." *Hmm. So Mother is on the same page as I am.* I nodded emphatically.

"And so I decided to speak with the servants about it, ask them some questions, and then…"

"And then?" There was strength in Mother's eyes. I leaned forward a little without even realizing it.

"It would seem that Keith has been somewhat depressed, unhappy as of late. Several servants reported witnessing him in such a state."

"Keith was… sad? Down?" I hadn't ever seen Keith looking like that. Had I simply not noticed?

"Yes. And from what I have been told, he only had such an expression after spending time with a certain person."

"Huh?! A certain person?" *But who? Who could it be? Is that person linked to Keith's troubles? Then we should speak to this person right away…* "But Mother, who is it?"

"…Well, you see…" Mother paused, before staring straight at me. "It is none other than YOU, Katarina!"

Her declaration made her sound like one of the famous detectives in the television programs I'd watched in my past life, in scenes where they point out the true perpetrator of a crime.

"…Huh?! M-Me?"

I could only gape in surprise as Mother continued, as if finally cornering the elusive criminal with her flawless deduction. "Yes, *you,*

Katarina. According to various testimonies I have received from the servants, Keith always seemed depressed after speaking to you."

"After speaking to me…" While I had been complaining to him quite often recently, was he ever depressed? Thinking back on it… hmm. Oh yes, there was that one day, right before we returned to the manor, when Keith made that sad face. "Ah, come to think of it…"

Before I could finish my sentence, my mother gave a deep sigh. "As I thought… so it was you." Just like a detective during a mystery's parlor scene. And then…

"The reason Keith ran away from home had nothing to do with inheriting the Claes name at all. The reason why he left… was due to the stress of having to clean up after you all the time!" Mother declared, her voice reaching a peak.

"Huh?! Clean up after me?" *Hmm. I suppose Keith has been supporting me and covering for me when I make mistakes, but… cleaning up after me?*

"I am sure he feels tired, having to look after his sloppy sister throughout all these years. But of course… Keith is such a gentle child. That is why he could not come clean with the facts. That is why he sent this letter…" Mother said sorrowfully, hanging her head as she did so.

"…" Well, the question of "cleaning up" after me aside, I supposed I had been barging into his room to complain a lot lately, and he'd had to put up with that. If that was what caused his apparent tiredness, then I could understand that. "…What do I do?" If Keith had really gotten tired of my antics and decided to never come home…

Seeing how deflated I was, Mother shot me a grave look, before gripping my hands tightly. "There is no use crying over spilled milk. Firstly, you shall sincerely apologize for everything you have done up until this point. And you shall inform your brother of how you will work hard and never trouble him again. If you sincerely communicate that to him, then Keith, being the gentle child he is… will surely forgive you."

"…M-Mother…" I was moved by her words. I could feel tears welling up in my eyes as I returned her grip with an equally earnest force. "Mother, I will apologize to Keith! And I'll tell him that I'll work hard not to trouble him again!"

"Yes, work hard indeed, Katarina!"

And so somewhere, in a room of Claes Manor, a very mismatched mother and daughter pair held each other's hands, shouting energetically.

Alright! We will now commence an insightful analysis on how we will get Keith to change his mind and return to Claes Manor.

Meeting chairwoman: Katarina Claes.

Meeting representative: Katarina Claes.

Meeting secretary: Katarina Claes.

"Well then. The subject of discussion for this particular meeting is the ways and methodologies with which we could convince Keith to return home. Everyone, let's hear your ideas."

"Yes. But as for ideas… wouldn't simply carrying out Mother's suggestion be enough? Like she said, we could just apologize and promise not to cause any more trouble."

"That's the basics of it, but I feel that we need to be more sincere in this kind of situation."

"Sincere?"

"For example, we could offer to do something for him, to make up for all the trouble we've caused up until now?"

"Oh ho, now that's a good suggestion. But what should we offer to do?"

"I haven't thought that far ahead!"

"That's not something to say so proudly, Miss Claes."

"Maybe a present of some kind? Or a treat?"

"I guess that would be fine, but would he be satisfied with just a treat?"

"Hmm, then how about new seeds or fertilizers?"

"That's what Katarina would want."

"In that case, then... how about I.O.U.s for shoulder massages or friendly back-washing in the shower?"

"Well, Father would like that kind of thing, but I don't know about Keith. Hmm, it isn't a bad suggestion though. It would be like an accumulation of the daily gratitude that we feel for him, represented by our actions."

"Well, it's decided then! We will apologize to Keith when we see him, and then express our gratitude with tangible actions."

"And also promise we won't cause him any more trouble!"

"Yes, definitely. For instance, no more eating too much and getting stomachaches, or rough housing indoors and breaking things. We should swear we'll be more aware of those things and not make the same mistakes."

"That's perfect. Well then... all that's left is to go talk to Keith."

"That's right!"

"So... where's Keith, again?"

"Ah!"

"Perhaps we should start by actually searching for him?"

"Words of wisdom indeed, Katarina Claes! That's just what we should do."

"Yes, first we should set off and search for him. If he went through all the effort of running away from home, it isn't likely that he's anywhere nearby. We may have to set out on a journey."

"A journey to find Keith! It's like that movie, *Something-Something In Search of Mother*!"

"Yes, but in this case it would be 'In Search of Keith' instead!"

"So then, our first course of action will be to set off in search of Keith. Are we all agreed?"

"Yes."

And so, I made up my mind to set off on a journey in search of my adopted younger brother.

Just after I'd resolved to go off and find Keith, news of my decision was quickly leaked. Before long, a bunch of people showed up wanting to come with me.

One of them was my fiancé, Jeord Stuart. "I shall come with you, Katarina, out of worry." I couldn't refuse.

The next was Larna, who somehow heard about this all the way at the Ministry. "It's a good opportunity, don't you think? Let me come with you. It'll be a good chance to train up new Ministry staff." Although I was surprised that Ministry employees went on excursions like this, having a big-shot like Larna with me would be helpful on the journey, so I took her up on her offer.

Also tagging along were the new staff that Larna had mentioned — Maria and Sora. The one who was now going by the name "Sora" was Rufus, the same person who had kidnapped me a while ago. Although he had used the Dark Arts to carry out a kidnapping, he had shed a lot of tears and portrayed himself as an unfortunate victim. *"My master made me do it!"* he'd claimed. Now he was in the Ministry's custody. Though Sora didn't really seem like the type to cry and claim he was threatened, from how he'd acted when he'd kidnapped me...

Anyway, that was how our motley crew — Jeord, Larna, Maria, Sora (Rufus), and me — set off on our journey in search of Keith.

"Come to think of it... there is something I would like to ask you, young miss," Anne said as she finished up her preparations for my upcoming journey. She was almost done with sorting out my hair and clothes. Although Anne usually accompanied me everywhere I went, she wouldn't be doing so this time. "I cannot help but be worried about you heading out on your own," she said in a somewhat severe tone.

Keith's disappearance hadn't been made public, and we had resolved to keep the search party relatively small as a result. Even so, we had quite the impressive roster. Larna, one of the strongest and most capable people in the Ministry, was with us. On top of that, we had a Wielder of Light and a Wielder of Darkness. And of course, a prince who could do just about anything. With this search party, given its unreasonably strong composition, I didn't think I had much to worry about.

I reassured Anne with those facts, but she was still hesitant. "I am referring to my worries about your daily life, young miss..."

Personally, I felt like I could take care of my own business. But Anne seemed to disagree. "You do not tidy your hair, nor do you iron out the wrinkles in your dresses! Whatever do you mean by taking care of yourself, young miss?!"

I mean... my hair's pretty silk anyway. It doesn't matter if it's a little messy. And as for my dresses, a few wrinkles here and there don't impact my ability to wear it. It'll be totally fine! "I'll make sure to do it right..." I said to Anne. But...

"That which you consider 'right,' young miss… is hardly appropriate for most situations…" This was Anne's response. What a terribly strict maid!

Even Jeord, who was a prince, wasn't accompanied by anyone. Having Anne along would be reassuring, but honestly, I would seem too sheltered if I alone brought along a servant. If possible, I wanted to go without any servants accompanying me.

My savior appeared in the form of Maria. "In that case, I shall assist Lady Katarina with her personal grooming," Maria said, smiling like a goddess.

Upon hearing her offer, Anne immediately agreed, quickly responding with, "If you would be so kind, Lady Maria." What a drastic difference from her earlier dismissal!

While the sudden change in Anne's attitude between talking to me and talking to Maria was less than ideal, in any case, I was able to avoid looking terribly sheltered and spoiled thanks to Maria. That said, Anne still helped me a lot and looked out for me as we prepared for the journey.

"Young miss, firstly… have you even decided on the direction of your search?"

"Huh? Direction?" I started gaping like a goldfish.

"You are on a search to locate Master Keith, yes? Then surely you would first have to head to a certain destination, or a location?"

"…Huh?" I froze up completely at Anne's question.

"…Um, young miss… have you not thought of where your search party would be headed toward, at all? Judging by how spirited you were and the volume of your declaration, and how all preparations had been completed… Did you perhaps not have a destination in mind from the start?"

"…"

"…Young miss."

Ah, Anne… please don't look at me with those eyes. I'm just as surprised as you. In my enthusiasm at the prospect of setting out on a journey in search of Keith, I had completely forgotten to even think of a destination.

Honestly, we didn't have a single clue about where Keith had gone. Perhaps he went west? East? North? South? I had no idea. Where were we even going, then…? *Hmm. What should I do?* The departure date was dangerously close.

What should I do?!

The next savior to appear was the Ministry big-shot herself. Larna soon fished me out of my predicament.

Although we were planning to leave very soon, I hadn't come up with a destination. I talked about it with Larna, who exploded into peals of laughter as she listened. Then she smiled with that cat-like smile of hers and said, "As expected of you, Katarina."

Then she said, "In that case, I do have something special for this occasion." She left, asking me to wait for a while. When she returned, she was holding what appeared to be some kind of plush toy. It had brown fur, round ears, and beady eyes. A stuffed bear?

"Um… Lady Larna. What's up with the toy?"

Larna responded with that same smile once more. "This is a magical tool — one we can use to locate Keith."

"A magical… tool?" It wasn't a phrase I'd heard before.

Larna provided an explanation while holding up the bear. Apparently, magical tools were the main subject of her research. She had made a great number of these tools, but said they were not very stable. She was still in the prototyping phase, apparently.

"If more advancements are made in the field of magical tool crafting, then we'll be able to grant the blessing of magic unto tools and objects..." Larna said, her eyes sparkling as she rambled on.

After that, Larna's passionate talk of magical tools went on for some time, eventually reaching a point of conceptual philosophy. I could only nod and respond with the occasional "Oh... I see."

As Larna continued on her impassioned explanation, I saw the plush toy next to her... move. *Wh-Wha?* I rubbed my eyes and stared once more... only for my gaze to meet with that of the stuffed bear's! Given that the bear had been put down with its head hanging downward... shouldn't it be looking down?! Why was it looking at me?

"Wh-Why?!" I blurted, surprised.

Larna soon followed my gaze. "Ah, yes. I was about to come to that," she said, once again holding up the plush bear. "This is something a certain weird— I mean, something a very *important* person in the kingdom asked me to make. It's a magical tool used to find people."

"A magical tool for... finding? People?"

"Yes indeed. You just have to strongly think of something of great value to the missing person, and you'll eventually pick up on their trail. It's useful for research into the Dark Arts as well, but..." Larna's explanation trailed off from there.

From what I understood, all I had to do was imagine a certain thing that was particularly important to Keith, mentally suggest that to the plush toy, and it would then magically show me where he had gone. According to Larna, its success rate was still somewhat varied at this point, but given that we had no clues, this tool was a lot better than nothing.

More importantly — "Um, Lady Larna... Did that plush bear just move?"

While Larna continued to speak, the plush toy seemed to squirm a little in her hands, moving this way and that. I couldn't help but notice.

"Ah, yes. It is, after all, a tool to locate people with. What good would it be if it couldn't move and lead the way?"

"What?! That plush toy will lead us to Keith?"

"That's right," Larna said, as if it were the most obvious thing in the world.

A plush toy that leads the way...? Well, I did wonder how a toy like that would be able to help us search. But a bear leading the way...? "Um. Why a plush toy, though?" I asked with a somewhat serious expression. Was there a deeper meaning to all this that I wasn't seeing?

"Ah. Because it's cute," Larna responded casually.

Huh?! That's the reason? Just because it's cute? Does its cuteness make it better somehow? I stared long and hard at the plush bear in Larna's arms. I'd been wondering ever since she returned with it... *Is this plush toy really cute? I feel like... it doesn't really look cute at all.*

Perhaps it would be a bit ironic for someone like me to say, given that I had the face of a villainess, but, this bear... it looked... ugly. Most plush toys are cute, but there was something about its face. Something about it was off. Where was this toy even found? I didn't say what I was thinking, but...

"Ah, I found it at a gift shop in town, you see. It was love at first sight," Larna said, smiling happily.

Ahem... to each their own, I suppose.

In any case, I guess we would now be using this strange-looking bear to search for Keith's whereabouts. In order to locate him, I needed something of value to him. So I returned to the manor and started searching for something that would fit the bill.

But hmm… What does Keith value? I had been with him all this time, but I couldn't think of anything. With that in mind, I decided to ask the servants who were usually in Keith's service.

"What Master Keith treasures? Hmm… Perhaps it would be something in this wooden chest?" The servant fetched me a large wooden chest from Keith's room. It was really fancy and ornamental for a chest. *Hmm, I've never seen this before.*

"Under normal circumstances, it would be most unbecoming to open something like this without Master Keith's permission, but we are in most pressing circumstances…"

"Thank you. I will apologize personally to Keith, don't worry about that."

The box was somewhat heavy. I placed it on a table and opened the lid. "Huh? This is…" I remembered these things. They were the birthday presents that I had given Keith, year after year. "Wow… even this, from all that time ago!" Among the items was a slip of paper with some childish handwriting on it that said: *"Whatever you wish for! Wish-granting ticket."* Judging by the writing, I was the one who had written it. But honestly, I didn't remember doing it.

He set all these things aside… it's so touching. Keith really did think a lot about his big sister!

Since I couldn't decide on which item would be the best, I ended up bringing the entire thing to Larna.

When I went to meet up with Larna again, I found one other person in her room.

"Well hello, Lady Katarina Claes."

I remembered this person and his flippant smile. It was Jeffrey Stuart, the first prince of the kingdom, and the older brother of both Jeord and Alan. *Huh? Why is the first prince here...?* In spite of my hesitation and mild shock, I still managed to issue a ladylike greeting in the way that noble society had taught me to.

As if reading my troubled expression, the still-smiling Prince Jeffrey glanced at me and said, "Actually, I asked Larna to develop a certain magical tool for me, and I am here to check on its progress, you see."

"A magical tool?" I hadn't even heard about magical tools until recently. Unlike me, Prince Jeffrey apparently knew enough to put in requests for them to be made. That made sense, him being royal, and all... *But I wonder what Prince Jeffrey asked for?* From what Larna had told me, there was a wide variety of magical tools.

"What kind of tool did you request?" I asked the prince.

It was Larna, however, who responded. "Ah, it is the tool for locating missing persons."

"Missing persons... Hm? So does that mean..." Although I wasn't the sharpest knife in the drawer, I picked up on that point somewhat quickly. *A magical tool for locating people... Isn't that the very same one that I was about to borrow? That ugly bear!*

"Yes. It's the tool that we'll be using during our journey," Larna said, still sounding casual.

Huh? Is it really okay for me to simply grab something the first prince requested? Wouldn't that be bad? I started to panic.

41

"Ah, there is no need to worry, Lady Katarina. I have already heard all about the matter," Jeffrey said, sounding as carefree as ever. "I am not really in a rush, you see. We don't really know how it would work, after all. Take this as its first run, and if it does work, I will use it next."

"...Is that so? Thank you, Prince Jeffrey."

The prince merely waved his hands this way and that. He didn't seem upset by me borrowing the tool at all. It would seem that our search party would be able to use it first without any issues.

Prince Jeffrey really didn't seem like royalty at all. Jeord and Alan didn't put on any airs either, although Alan was pretty haughty in his younger days. Even so, neither of them had that carefree, casual atmosphere that Prince Jeffrey had about him.

I had met him at the school festival, and according to Anne, Prince Jeffrey was seen as a very respectable person and had a large political following. But I couldn't quite make a connection with that image now that I was here and speaking to him in person. I suddenly realized that I was staring at him.

"Hmm?" He just responded with that same friendly, flippant smile.

"U-Um... if I may ask, Prince Jeffrey, what do you intend to use that magical tool to do?" I couldn't tell him that he didn't seem like a royal, so the question just slipped out before I thought about it. But then it occurred to me that this probably wasn't an appropriate question to ask someone who I barely knew. Perhaps it was for some really important mission on behalf of the throne. I started to feel uneasy as I thought about it.

"Hmm! Well, you see... I'd just like to know where the ones I love the most are at all times!"

"Th-The ones you love most?"

"Yes, the ones I love most in the whole world, indeed! I'd like to know where they are… all the time."

"…Is that… some mission you're doing for the kingdom?"

"Hardly! It has nothing to do with that, actually. This tool is meant for my personal use."

…So it has nothing to do with the kingdom, I see. Even so, there's something weird about his line of reasoning. To know where the ones he loves the most are at all times… Wouldn't that make him some kind of stalker? Hmm. No… I should stop thinking too deeply about this. I felt like I could see something truly terrifying behind this flippant prince's smile.

I quickly erased the thoughts in my mind and changed the subject. "Well then… with your permission, Prince Jeffrey, we will use it first."

"Why yes! Of course, of course," the prince replied, with that smile still plastered across his features.

With the prince's permission obtained, I handed Larna the wooden box I had taken all the way from Claes Manor, only for her to raise her voice in surprise as she lifted its lid. "What… is all this?"

I figured she'd be surprised, given that she hardly had any context. "These are all presents I've given to Keith. It would seem that he treasured each and every last one of them."

At my words, Prince Jeffrey, who had been peeking into the box beside Larna, had something to say too. "This… is quite something," he said, sounding impressed. "He treasured all your gifts this much… they must really mean a lot to him."

"Treasured?" I asked, unsure of what the prince meant.

He smiled at me meaningfully. "Well yes, Lady Katarina. This means that he treasures you that much."

43

"Yes… he really does appreciate his sister," I responded with a smile of my own, only for Prince Jeffrey and Larna to shoot me strange looks. *Hmm? Did I say something weird?*

According to Larna, the object of value that the plush toy needed had to be presented to it at regular intervals, so something I could easily take along with me would be best. With that in mind, we isolated several contenders from the box. In the end, we chose an embroidered handkerchief that I had given Keith a long time ago.

Honestly, I had forgotten about it completely, but Keith had kept it in very good condition. It had been beautifully preserved; there wasn't even a speck of dirt on it. We decided to present it to the plush toy.

"How do we have the bear remember this item?" I asked.

Larna merely flashed me a confident, anticipatory smile as she handed the handkerchief to the bear. "Just watch and see."

The plush bear, which had apparently gained the ability to move after becoming a magical tool, soon nodded, accepting the handkerchief. It brought it close to its nose — which was just a button of some kind, by the way — and started sniffing it.

Huh?! It's sniffing like a dog would? Actually, do plush toys even have a sense of smell?! I could only watch on, stunned, as the bear did its thing. It handed the item back to Larna, nodding in a way that suggested it was aware of its actions.

"Um… Lady Larna. Will this really help us in our search…?"

"Yes, perfectly. Alright, Alexander, tell us where Keith is."

"Eh…? Alexander?"

"Yes, it's this bear's name. It's a cool name, if I do say so myself."

"I… see…" I no longer understood if Lady Larna wanted a cute bear or a cool one. In any case, it didn't fit a bear as ugly as this one!

I suppressed my feelings about it as Alexander the plush bear stood up and pointed in the eastern direction of the room.

"Oh, Alexander! Well done!" Larna said, seemingly impressed.

Slowly, I turned my eyes toward the bear, unsettled by its behavior... only to see it glance ever so slightly in my direction, and then, as if to mock me, do a little "Harumph."

...For some reason, I felt that Alexander the Ugly Bear and I would not get along.

In any case, now that we at least had a direction to work with, as pointed out by the Ugly Bear (I really didn't want to call it "Alexander"), our plans were more or less decided, and we prepared to set out right on schedule.

All I had to do was wait at the academy's gates for the arrival of Larna and Sora from the Ministry. Also gathered here were Mary, Alan, Sophia, and Nicol.

"*Sniff*... I wish I could go with you as well, Lady Katarina..." Mary said with a lonely look on her face.

"Nothing we can do about it this time, you know," said Alan, Mary's fiancé, as he offered her some words of comfort.

"Me too, Lady Katarina..." Sophia also seemed very sad. She was practically being propped up by Nicol, who was standing behind her.

I would have liked to take everyone along too, but that would make our group too large. And also...

"It would be unthinkable for members of the student council to simultaneously vanish during this busy time." At Nicol's words, Sophia's expression became one of determination, and Mary's brow furrowed.

"It is as Master Nicol says. At this busy time, when the graduation ceremony is so near... to think that the president himself would be away! Unbelievable," Mary said as she leveled a stern gaze in Jeord's general direction.

But Jeord merely responded, "But you see, most of my work has already been squared away. Consider that Nicol is with you — if anything were to happen, I am sure he would offer his assistance. You are all but prepared." He sounded completely carefree. On the other hand...

"I-I'm sorry... to be stepping away at such a crucial time..." Maria said, beginning to apologize frantically.

Mary started becoming flustered at the sight of this. "Ah, but your presence is needed for this particular event! Please pay it no heed..." she said desperately.

Having escaped from Mary's clutches, Jeord immediately approached me, holding my hand in his. "I will make sure to protect you, Katarina." He smiled faintly.

"...R-Right..." *Why is he getting so close to me so quickly?* I thought as I replied in an absent-minded fashion. I noticed Jeord's expression change. *Hmm? What was it?*

"C-Could this be..." For some reason Jeord, who was always calm and collected, seemed terribly shaken.

Nicol interjected with his usual calm demeanor. "She has forgotten, most likely. She probably has nothing but Keith's safety on her mind."

"Hm?" *What are they going on about now?*

"It is as you say... there was, after all, that one incident where she forgot a string of recent events and thought of it as a dream — but to think that she would be... to this extent..." For some reason, Jeord's shoulders slumped.

Mary had been listening to the conversation from the side. She was in such a bad mood before, but she started smiling again almost immediately. And then there was me, Katarina Claes, with an almost-visible question mark floating above my head.

"Ah, it is nothing, Lady Katarina. Please, pay it no heed." Maria flashed me one of the best smiles I had seen to date.

How am I not supposed to think about it? Well... if Maria says it's fine, I guess I can let it go.

Before long, Larna and Sora arrived.

"It is good to see you again, Lady Katarina." The person who said this while bowing was a blue-haired, playboy-looking young man. I hadn't seen Sora since the kidnapping incident. He still had the same smile, but I did notice one difference — he was now speaking very formally to me.

"Yes, it's good to see you too—"

As I responded, Jeord darted between us, positioning himself in front of me. "Ah, Master Sora, yes? It is a pleasure to meet you." He flashed Sora one of his fairy-tale prince smiles.

"Oh, just Sora is fine, Prince Jeord. The pleasure is all mine, I'm sure." Such was Sora's polite response... but for some reason, I could feel tension sparking in the air. Perhaps I was just imagining things?

"Sorry to keep you waiting! Well then, since we are all present, I suppose we should be off," Larna said, oblivious and impervious to the tension in the air.

With a few goodbyes and waves, I said my farewells to my friends, and our little party set off on our journey in search of Keith.

When I awoke, I found myself in a room I'd never seen before. I could not move my arms or legs. From what I could see, I had been bound with rope, and was laid down on a bed. It was obviously not a normal situation.

I remembered following the woman who invited me into an alleyway... and my memories stopped short there. From that point on, my recollections were hazy. Perhaps some things happened... perhaps they did not. I could not remember a thing.

I deeply regretted blindly following after that woman. To begin with, she was really good for nothing. I should have learned that lesson a long time ago. I suppose it was because I had been living happily all this time. Because I was always with my sister, and was influenced by her... I had started doubting people less.

In any case... endlessly regretting my circumstances would get me nowhere. Firstly, I had to confirm my situation. Just as I started to look around, the only door to the room opened. A man I had never seen before entered.

Upon noticing that I had woken up, his eyes narrowed and he walked toward me slowly. "Been a while." The man walked up to the bed and looked at me with a twisted smile on his face. Messy hair, a seemingly endless amount of flesh on all parts of his body — to the point where even his face was almost buried under it. His skin shone under the tension of fat under skin, and I could see rolls of it escaping his clothing.

This man... I did not remember ever meeting such a person. That was why I thought it was best to remain silent and see what he would do. Perhaps that upset him. The man's face seemed more and more displeased.

"Yeah, don't say anything, then. Guess you don't want to say anything to lower-class nobles, huh!" He practically spat out his words in his rage, and that revived some old memories. Memories of my childhood… one of the boys who was raised in the same place as I was.

"…Thomas?"

The moment I said that word, a streak of pain flashed across my face. The man, now red-faced, had apparently swung his fist at me.

"D-Don't you dare… someone like you… say my name so freely! SOMEONE LIKE YOU!" The man known as Thomas raised his fist once more, striking me. Although he now looked completely different from his younger self… yes, he was just like how he used to be.

With my arms and legs restrained, all I could do was endure the beating. *Ah. An almost nostalgic sensation.* Back then, I always held it in. Endured it. I would close off my heart and wait for the storm to pass. It had been a while since I'd felt anything like it. I had never crossed paths with this feeling since.

As I hazily entertained those thoughts and looked at Thomas, who was still railing on me, in an equally hazy way… I became aware of a woman standing behind him. Her black hair had no order to it — it just flowed. She appeared to be almost the same age as I was.

Her form naturally drew my eyes to it. It wasn't because she was stunning, or beautiful, or anything like that. It was because she was smiling. She was smiling as the red-faced man before me continued pummeling his fists into my body.

Her innocent smile sent shivers down my spine. I felt an intense sense of fear — not of this man who was hitting me, but the woman who smiled as she watched. Perhaps she sensed my gaze, as her eyes soon met mine. Those eyes were innocent, like a child's.

Ah… what will become of me? Will I never see her again? I thought… as the smile of the woman I loved most in the world floated into my mind.

The journey in search of Keith had begun. Trailing Keith's scent (well, more like his memories, I suppose. One cannot see smells, after all), the carriage advanced steadily in the direction Ugly Bear had pointed out.

To keep things simple, our group was advancing in the direction indicated by the bear, and that was that. As for whether this bear truly knew where it was going… well, all we could do now was place our hopes in it.

The carriage we were in was somewhat large. We had chosen a model usually used by merchants and the common folk. Six people could fit inside easily, and we only had five. Sora was acting as the coachman, so he wasn't even in the carriage at all.

Shortly after we set off, Maria had a question for Larna — something about magic, I guess. This conversation went on for a while and still showed no signs of ending. Maybe because Maria asked her question first and felt some sort of obligation to keep the conversation going, she continued listening to Larna's passionate explanation with a serious expression on her face.

It seemed like Jeord, who was sitting in the row of seats in front of me, hadn't been in a good mood since we'd left. He was quieter than usual, and though he had a smile on his face when he engaged in casual conversation, it was fainter than usual.

As for me, while I had originally been listening to Larna, the conversation's contents were a little beyond me, and I soon started dozing off.

"Katarina, we're at the first town."

Larna's voice shook me awake from my sleep. I opened my eyes and peered outside the window. As she said, we were now in a large town. We'd already arrived at the first town in this direction while I was asleep.

With Larna's prompting, I finally got off the carriage, and the hum of the town soon filled my ears. Although this was the closest town from where we had set off, the carriage had traveled for a good half a day. This was the first time I had been to this place. I could feel a small spring of excitement well up from within me.

First, we'd have to make some inquiries about Keith's whereabouts in this town.

"This town is big, and a large group would only attract attention. We'll split into three smaller groups: Katarina and me, Jeord and Maria, and Sora," Larna suggested.

But Jeord immediately protested. "If possible, I would very much like to go with Katarina…"

Larna, however, dismissed him almost immediately. "This arrangement is set in stone," she said, and that was that.

Well, I didn't really mind. Anyone was fine, as long as I was with someone. I'd just get lost on my own, after all, so it would be better for me to have at least one other person with me.

So I ended up sticking with Larna. As we made our rounds around town, I realized that this place wasn't too different from the area I lived in, probably because they were still reasonably close to each other. Even so, I had never been here before, and couldn't help but ogle my surroundings.

Seeing this, Larna chuckled slightly with a hint of exasperation on the side. "You're almost like some village girl seeing a real town for the first time."

Looking kind of like tourists, the two of us went around town and asked for information on Keith. But we didn't find anything. Honestly, I thought Keith was very handsome, putting aside my perspective as his sister. I'd set off on this journey thinking that he'd be easy to find — a few questions, and that'd be it. The fact that we still found no trace of him was disheartening.

Seeing my mood drop, Larna turned to me. "But we've only just started, Katarina. We still have a ways to go, right? Come now, don't make that face," she reassured me. "Also, the location Alexander was pointing at still seems somewhat far away," she added, pointing to the bear on her shoulder.

As I turned to look at the bear, it gave me that look again — that "harumph," like it was making fun of me! As I expected, this bear was… unbearable.

Noticing my reaction, Larna turned to look at the bear, only for it to return to its usual, unremarkable expression. *What an irritating thing!*

My annoyance soon faded though. As we turned the corner, a shop with tasty-looking foods on display came into view, and with that, my irritation vanished with a poof.

"Wow! These look delicious!" I found myself plastered onto the shop window before I knew it — the normal effect of spotting food. After all, I did really, really love snacking. *In fact, that over there… I've never seen anything like it before. I wonder what it tastes like?*

As I continued staring at the shop display, I felt myself slowly getting hungry. Soon, my stomach erupted into low-pitched, audible growls. What can I say? I suppose my body is honest about its desires.

I heard laughter from behind me. I turned and came face to face with Larna, who seemed to think that this was all quite hilarious. She probably heard my stomach rumblings. Quite clearly, too.

Larna kept laughing for a while, before finally she said, "Well, there's still some time before we gather up again. Want to buy some food and have a bite on the way back?"

Of course! "Yes!" I replied happily.

I entered a sweets shop with Larna and bought all kinds of stuff for myself, including the unfamiliar treat I saw before. I felt guilty about only feeding myself though, so I ended up getting some of the shopkeeper's recommendations for everyone else too. Larna herself didn't seem hungry, so I just bought plenty for us all to have in the future.

After that, we were finally able to rest on a bench in the town plaza, and I quickly opened up the bag of snacks in my hands.

"Delicious…!"

I wasted no time, quickly stuffing my face with my recent purchases. As the different delicious tastes spread through me, I noticed Larna laughing to herself in that fashion again.

"What's wrong?" *Huh? My stomach isn't rumbling anymore, is it?*

"Ah, sorry. I couldn't help myself, Katarina. Seeing your myriad of expressions, I just end up laughing."

"I… see." *Is she praising me? Hmm. I'm not sure.*

"It just means that I have a ball when I'm with you. I finally understand how they feel now. I suppose you are an irreplaceable person to them in many ways…"

"…Them who?" *I wonder what she's talking about?* I thought I'd ask just to be sure, but Larna merely smiled vaguely and stayed silent, not answering me.

"It's very much like how magic is to me." That was her only response.

"How magic is to you, Lady Larna…?"

"Yes, magic itself was what brought color to my world, you see," Larna said, her calm expression suggesting a hint of nostalgia. Then she continued, "I was very tired with the world from a young age. I was very skilled and could do most things with ease. I didn't view anything as fun or enjoyable. I was an insufferable child, you know? One that always felt a pervading sense of boredom. I wasn't very cute at all."

I felt like I had heard of someone else like this before. Someone who was lonely because they were blessed with perfection — someone with no hobbies or interests.

"However… someone came along. They gifted me with a large collection of books on magic. This person was quite a strange one. They were not books that children could read, much less understand. In fact, even adults had a hard time understanding these tomes."

Hmm, giving books on magic to a child… If I had been given something like that, those books would have immediately gone to their graves in the depths of my bookshelves.

Naturally, Larna was different. "I tried reading the books a little, and was immediately hooked. At first, I thought they were interesting, which made me want to read through all of them at once. There were so many of them though, so I only finished reading them on the second, hmm, perhaps third day. When I was finally done, I was enamored with this little thing called magic. Fortunately, I was born with magical aptitude myself, and was able to test certain things out. That only made me more interested, of course."

I see. And this was how Larna became the magic otaku she is today. I nodded as I continued listening.

"Come to think of it, you're only the second person I've told this to, Katarina," Larna said.

"Huh? Is that so?" I had assumed that this was something that could simply be told to anyone.

"Well, no one wants to listen to things like this. The only ones who have listened were you, Katarina... and my partner."

"Buddy...?"

"That's right. My fiancé."

"Your fiancé?!" I was surprised. To think that Larna, who was only interested in magic, would have a fiancé! *Well, I did hear from Raphael that Larna is a noble of somewhat high standing... so I suppose this is possible to a certain extent.*

"Wh-Who is he?" Curious, I posed the question to Larna, only for her to answer me with a single phrase:

"A weirdo."

Ah, I suppose she's gotten his character type down...

I see... but Larna's fiancé, huh? It could be a little scary, but I was curious enough to want to see him at least once. *Fiancé... hmm. Come to think of it...*

"Ah! I remember now!"

"Wh-What is it, all of a sudden?" Larna seemed taken aback at my sudden outburst.

"Ah, sorry Lady Larna. Speaking about your childhood reminded me of someone. I felt like I'd heard something similar before, and now I finally remember."

"Oh? And who would that be?"

"Ah, yes. It's Prince Jeord. He's capable of anything, and has no dreams or aspirations at all... at least, that's what I heard." I didn't hear that directly from him, of course. This was all from me reading the scenario of *Fortune Lover* in my previous life.

"I see. So Prince Jeord was the same way? Then I suppose he has safely managed to find something that allows him to dream as well."

"...? Well no, not quite... I don't think Prince Jeord has found anything like that just yet."

After all, Jeord was supposed to meet with Maria, fall in love, and all that. Unfortunately, that never happened, and that was why I thought that Jeord had yet to find this thing that allowed him to have dreams and aspirations.

"...I suppose this really is unrequited."

"Hm?"

Larna sighed deeply, though I didn't know why. "Anyway, finding something that inspires you to dream is a wonderful thing. Just one thing, and suddenly color and beauty floods your vision. You start to see things differently. Everything becomes more enjoyable, and you find yourself becoming happier and happier, like I am now," Larna said before smiling at me like a mischievous kid.

Then she added, "Alright, it's almost that time. We should return to the carriage." So we made our way back, with me holding a bag of snacks in one hand.

Upon seeing me return with the bag, Jeord turned to me and said, "I hope you are not only eating sweets and nothing else, Katarina..." And with that, my amount of souvenir snacks was reduced.

As for Jeord's share, he offered it to Maria, who was very pleased. "Wow, this looks delicious!" she exclaimed.

No one in our party had any leads with regard to Keith, so we soon piled into the carriage, and were once again on our way.

As I cheerfully ate the snacks I'd bought, I got lost in conversation, and before long we were at the next town. We were pretty far from the academy grounds, and this town was much bigger than the last.

"Wow! It's so big!" I exclaimed, peering out of the carriage window.

"It is. It's the largest town in the region, in fact," Larna replied. "In any case, it's already late in the day. Perhaps we should rest here tonight."

It was decided that we would be spending the night in this town. As we got out of the carriage and walked into the town's streets, we were greeted with a busy sight. Not quite as busy as the areas around the royal castle, but busy nonetheless. There were several times the number of people compared to the previous town, and many more shops too. From what I was told, Larna and Sora had been here before, but this was the first time for the other members of our party.

It was a day of firsts for me. I had never been to the town we were previously in either. Still, it had been relatively close to where I grew up, and so it featured similar sights, shops, and such. This town, though, was completely different.

The atmosphere was different, and there were many objects I had never seen before on sale. My eyes shifted from one storefront to the other, peering at the seemingly endless array of items that were on display.

Before I knew it, my flitting eyes had settled on a certain object. "Wah! This is cool! It looks so nice! I want one!"

"Katarina. I should remind you that we are not here on a leisure trip," Jeord said, appropriately reprimanding me for my overly tourist-like mentality.

"Ugh… that's right…"

"But… hmm. If it does catch your fancy, perhaps I will purchase one for you. Which one of these items is it?"

"Huh?! Really?!" *Our prince is truly generous!*

I was the daughter of a duke, yes, but whenever I wanted to buy things my parents would always say *"It would be unbecoming of you to spend needlessly, Katarina,"* and decrease my allowance. So I had no choice but to be somewhat strict with the things I bought. Honestly, most of my funds went to saplings, seeds, or fertilizers, so I was usually short on money that I could freely spend. In fact, I'd already spent most of my allowance on treats at the previous town. With that in mind, I had to be more conservative with my funds from here on out. In that case… it made sense to take Jeord up on his offer!

Without wasting any more time, I enthusiastically pointed out a certain item to Jeord. "This one right here, Prince Jeord!"

"Ah?! Th-This is…" Jeord seemed to physically pull away from the storefront. After a while, he asked, "Do tell, Katarina, what exactly is this?"

"I have no idea. It looks cool though, doesn't it? Look at it!" I replied.

The object that had caught my eye, and that I was now holding in my hand, was a round tool about the size of my palm. I guess you could assume it was a pocket mirror at first glance, but it didn't have a mirror of any kind. It seemed like a decorative item with a circular depression that contained an ornamental object. I had no idea what the strange disc was for. It looked like some kind of secret, stealthy magical tool, like that Ugly Bear.

Whatever it was, I thought it was really cool. I almost felt like I could shout "COME FORTH!" and summon a mythical beast of some sort on command. The way it looked stoked the flames of my otaku soul from my past life and made me want this object very badly. With that in mind, I tried my hardest to express to Jeord its innate coolness and explain why I wanted it.

But Jeord only responded with a vague, "I… see." Then he continued, "In any case, we should really ask the shopkeep what this… item is used for." This was his sensible response, and so we did just that.

"Ah, good sir. This is a decorative item. An ornament of sorts," the old shopkeeper replied.

"Just an ornament? Did some famous craftsman in the region create it?" Jeord asked.

The shopkeep seemed a little unsettled by the question. "Unfortunately, good sir, I have no idea who made the item in question. It came into my possession from the inventory of other shops. No one wanted to purchase it! It has been sitting in my store for quite a time too, and few have shown interest in it. I was just about to let it go as well, if I may say so…"

Apparently, this strange disc didn't sell no matter where it went — it would always be left behind in a shop's inventory, and ended up being passed on from one shop to the other. This man had received it from another shopkeep he was friends with for that exact reason.

As a result, it was on sale for a cheap price. Although Jeord had so generously offered to purchase the disc for me, I was relieved that it didn't cost very much.

"Is this price… really alright?" Jeord asked again and again.

The shopkeep, however, merely responded with, "Yes, good sir, this will do," without fail.

"Thank you very much, Prince Jeord," I said, happily thanking Jeord as I tucked the strange ornamental disc away in my pocket.

"But… such a cheap item, Katarina? Would it not have been more fitting if you chose something more expensive?" he said.

"Nah! After all, you've been buying all kinds of saplings and seeds and things for me all this time! Those are expensive, so I feel bad!"

"You should hardly be bothered by those gifts, Katarina. You are my fiancée after all, are you not?"

"Eh, but that…" I was Jeord's fiancée, yes. But that was temporary, wasn't it? Surely Jeord would find someone he actually liked sometime later. *Hmm… why do I feel like I've forgotten something important, ever since I found out that Keith ran away from home?*

As I stood lost in thought, Jeord extended a hand, stroking my hair. For some reason, my heartbeat became audibly louder.

"Say, Katarina… perhaps you have forgotten. Perhaps your mind is filled with thoughts of Keith. But as I had said before…"

"Ah, yes. Just when I thought I had not seen the two of you for a bit. But here you are, whiling away the time." That voice came from Sora, who had appeared out of nowhere and grabbed Jeord's hand. With it gone from my hair, I quickly forgot all about the thing I thought I would recall.

"…Sora. Did you do that on purpose?" Jeord said, turning to Sora with a grave, hostile expression. He had been smiling up until just now, but now Jeord's mood took an immediate turn for the worse for some reason.

But… why? He was all happy and smiling until a moment ago!

"Yes. I have been tasked with it, after all," Sora answered.

"Tasked, you say…?" Jeord's expression of surprise did nothing to Sora's unwavering smile.

"Yes. A request from Lady Mary Hunt through the Ministry, you see. To 'ensure Lady Katarina Claes's safety.' And so there you have it."

"And… does that include getting in my way?"

"Yes. If anything, that would be the core of the request in question, Prince Jeord."

"…" Jeord's expression darkened even further, but he did not speak.

Although there were sections of the conversation I didn't understand, it would seem like Mary had put in a formal request with the Magical Ministry to ensure my safety during this search. I felt happy — it wasn't exactly a dangerous trip, and yet my friends cared enough about me to do something like that. I really was blessed with gentle and caring friends.

"Well then. We have found a place to rest for the night. Let us make our way there. Lady Larna and Lady Maria are waiting for us."

We started following Sora, but Jeord kept mumbling to himself. Something like, "To think that she would go this far…" and, "I've been outdone…"

Hmm, I don't know what that could be about. Did something happen?

Apparently, Sora was the one who had recommended this inn to us. He really was dependable.

There were two rooms — Larna, Maria, and I shared one, while Jeord and Sora shared the other. "We do apologize that we could not provide individual rooms… there's a bit of a room shortage tonight, you see," said the staff at the inn.

Honestly, I was happy. This reminded me of the school trips I had in my previous life. I always slept alone in my room normally, so maybe that was why I felt a surge of excitement as I entered the room.

"Could I have this bed over here?" I asked hesitantly. The others agreed, and I immediately dove onto it. I wouldn't be able to do anything like this under normal circumstances, since Anne would get upset at me. But the excitement of feeling like I was on a school trip made me forget about that.

Maria seemed surprised upon witnessing my bed-dive, but Larna smiled and said, "Seems like you're having fun!" The bear, which was standing next to her, however… gave me that snort again, complete with a mocking expression. I really couldn't bring myself to like this bear.

With our room planning done, we headed toward the dining area for a meal. Dishes I had never seen before were laid out before me, and soon I was happily having my meal with everyone else. In my excitement…

"Ah, this looks delicious too! That over there as well! Ah… but this one…!"

…It seemed that I had a little too much to eat. Although Jeord did give me a somewhat half-hearted warning of "Katarina. Eating too much will give you a stomachache, yes?", my excitement stopped me from heeding his advice.

If Keith were here, he would say, *"Surely you have had enough to eat, Big Sister."* And with that, he would confiscate the dishes laid out before me… But Keith wasn't here now. As a result, my stomach was terribly full when we finally returned to our rooms, to the point where it was a little difficult to move around.

Jeord gave me his usual exasperated expression, since he'd warned me before. But the bear shot me an ice-cold stare, as if it were saying *"Hmph. You fool."*

I guess I should be more careful next time. Although I somehow managed to return to my room, it was difficult to stay standing — all I could do was lie down on my bed and wait for my stomach to finish digesting my dinner.

Honestly, I should have been engaging in an enjoyable girl-talk session with Maria right now… but my stomach hurt far too much. I couldn't possibly talk in this state. *Ah, how sad.*

As I lay there with my hands on my uncomfortably full belly, Larna suddenly spoke up. "I have some matters to attend to, and so I'll be stepping out for a while." And with that, she was gone. Night-time sightseeing tours, perhaps…?

Although I hugged my belly and complained for a while, I eventually fell asleep. When I opened my eyes again, the room was already dark, lit only by the faint light of the oil lamp in the room. Larna was still out, it would seem. Even Maria was resting in her bed.

Maria had already changed into her sleep clothes, a loose nightgown. In the lamp's dim glow, her golden-blonde hair seemed wispier than usual. She somehow looked different — she was exuding an air of sensuality that I couldn't explain.

Before I knew it, I was entranced by the sight of her. It didn't take Maria long to notice my gaze, and she soon turned around to face me.

"I see you are awake, Lady Katarina? Is your stomach feeling better?" Maria asked, with the expression of an angel.

I blushed in spite of myself. "Yes, I'm fine! Totally! No issues whatsoever!" I replied, almost bolting out of bed as I did so.

"I'm relieved," Maria replied with a faint smile.

As I stared at her smiling face, I became increasingly convinced of the fact that Maria was the most charming woman in the world. I had felt that way about her lovable nature when I first met her at the academy. I was surprised then. But being so close to Maria now... I felt the pull of her charm increasing.

At first, I'd thought that this was a given for the protagonist for an otome game. *Of course she would be born with the best specs,* I thought... but that wasn't quite it. Maria worked hard for what she had. She wasn't born with everything just because she was the protagonist. When I had noticed that, I saw her in a renewed light — she was even more amazing than before.

She was gentle, considerate, caring, and hardworking... I really did like her. If I were a man, I would take Maria as my bride without question. With that in mind... how did the game end with that friendship ending, of all things? It was a mystery even to me. How could it be that no one showed any interest in her, as impressive and amazing as she was? Given her nature, a reverse harem ending wouldn't come across as strange to me at all.

Were the men around me really so blind to Maria's splendor? Or was it because they didn't know how to approach her, and were just hanging back as a result? If that were the case, I'd be happy to discuss it with them and even provide advice. Although I had zero experience with love in my previous life, I had read many manga and played many otome games. Combined with all the romance novels I had read in this life, I was sure that I had plenty of valuable advice to offer.

Though no one ever approached me with regard to love — not in my previous life, and not in my current one either. Even if I asked direct questions during our girl-talk sessions, all my friends would say, "We like you, Lady Katarina." With that, they would deflect the question. I suppose I really wasn't destined to experience love in the third dimension.

But today, of all days, was a sleepover! I made up my mind. Today would be the day I had a serious, no-holds-barred girl-talk session with Maria! *Alright, let's do this, Katarina Claes!*

"Um, Maria… Huh? Maria, what are you doing?" Just as I had steeled my resolve and prepared myself for the long-awaited girl-talk… I turned to Maria, only to find her busy at work.

"Ah, yes… just some touch-ups for this little one here…" Maria pointed at the Ugly Bear, which was currently sprawled out across her knees. It would seem that she had been busy giving the bear a good clean. It was grinning widely, as if it were enjoying itself. The more Maria cleaned it up, the more its expression became one of utter satisfaction.

"It's really cute, isn't it?" Maria said, continuously stroking the bear's surface, almost lovingly. Although the bear's face was ugly, the way it behaved (around others, at least) was somewhat cute. Apparently Maria was absolutely taken with the thing.

The bear seemed incredibly pleased as Maria continued stroking it as it laid on her knees, curling up against her hand this way and that. It was acting cute. I found this really annoying, for some reason… And then, the bear's eyes and mine met.

"Heh. Envious, aren't you?" the bear's expression seemed to say.

…Oh, yes. Very annoying. What was with this thing anyway, ever since the first time it met me?! It was cute and lovable to everyone else! Why did it act this way toward me and only me? The difference was way too stark!

I glared at the bear with all my might. But Maria seemed to misunderstand my intense stare.

"Ah, I suppose you'd like to touch it as well, Lady Katarina. Here you go," she said, offering the bear to me.

No, Maria. I do not want this thing. Although I was happy that she was being so considerate, I could not see this bear as cute — not in the slightest. But I couldn't say that to Maria, not with her arms outstretched and that smile on her face. I accepted the bear, for now.

Once it was at an angle where Maria couldn't see its face, the bear shot me an indignant glare. *Hmph. You lousy bear. Even I don't want to be doing this.* But the bear decided to play along, and was now sitting quietly on my knee.

Maria left for the washroom a while later. As soon as she was out of sight, the bear leapt off me, before frantically brushing its behind with its stubby arms, as if it had been sitting on something foul.

This thing's attitude is the worst. Not to be defeated, I also rapidly brushed off where the bear had been sitting with my hand. With that, the bear regarded me with an expression of pity, before seemingly sighing as it slumped its arms.

"Wh-What is it with you?! What's with your attitude?!" I shouted in spite of myself. The bear, however, merely intensified its condescending gaze. It seemed very different from the lovable, cute plush toy that had been wriggling on Maria's knees earlier.

The bear and I then entered into a staring match — although I was the only one really staring. The bear merely looked in my general direction with that irritating, condescending gaze. This went on for a while, until Maria finally returned to the room.

Seeing that the bear had distanced itself from me and was now on my bed, she asked innocently, "Hmm? Lady Katarina, are you already done with the bear?"

"Yes, I've had quite enough."

And with that, the bear returned to Maria. "Well then, perhaps I should hug this little one to sleep tonight…" Maria hugged it tight, and the bear responded with a happy, pleased expression.

The speed it changed its attitude was frightening… to think that it had been looking down on me mere moments ago! It didn't seem like anything but some cute mascot character right now. *It's really good at that innocent front, huh… what are you, a cat?* No… it was a bear. A lousy bear.

In the end, Maria slipped into bed while hugging the bear. I changed into my pajamas too and burrowed back into my bed.

"Heehee…"

"What is it, Maria?" A while after I had gotten into bed, Maria's adorable laughter crept into my ears.

"I'm just happy, Lady Katarina…" she replied.

"Happy?" *Why? Is it the bear? Is it because she went to bed hugging it? Why does Maria like that lousy bear so much?!* That terrible, innocence-feigning, rotten-on-the-inside bear…

"Yes. I had no friends ever since my magic manifested itself, so I've never slept in the same room as someone else before, except for family. So I'm just… happy."

Ah, so it's that? I found my intense dislike for the bear burning hot in my chest before I had even heard her out.

"…Ah. My apologies… I should not be saying such inconsiderate things during this tenuous time, with Master Keith missing…" Maria said apologetically.

"I think it's fun too," I admitted, and that was enough for Maria to start laughing softly again. I was happy that Maria and I felt the same way.

"Hey, this doesn't have to be the only time! We should go on a trip again together. Next time we'll invite Mary and Sophia too."

Maria immediately responded with a "yes." But after a while, she spoke up again. "...Lady Katarina. I... before I met you at the academy, I always got into bed at night feeling incredibly lonely. But.. things are really fun now. I cannot help but be happy."

Although Maria had made many friends and was enjoying her life now, she had a hard time before she entered the academy, considering her social standing and everything. It was a really good thing that she was happy now. All's well that ends well.

"And so... the fact that I can be like this right now... it's all thanks to you, Lady Katarina."

"Oh!" *Huh? Thanks to me? But why? Is she sleep-talking? Is she already half-asleep after slipping into her sheets?* "Wh-What are you talking about, Maria? How could that be? You are where you are because of your own hard work! I didn't do anything!" I responded in a panic to Maria's sleep-talk.

In the dimly lit room, Maria's cheeks seemed slightly reddened. For some reason, her eyes seemed to be glistening too. *Hm? It is because she yawned? What about her red cheeks, though?*

"...Lady Katarina. Please... stay by my side forever," Maria said, staring straight at me with her soft, glistening eyes. It was almost like a confession of love — I felt my own cheeks getting hot.

"...Yes. Of course," I replied, my voice slightly quivering. Maria's charm was impressive indeed. If I continued talking with her like this while looking deep into her eyes, I had a feeling that I would really set foot into a forbidden world.

I laid back down and closed my eyes. As soon as I did so, the excitement of the day and the tiredness I had been holding at bay hit me all at once, and before I knew it, I was fast asleep. In the end, I had no idea when Larna finally returned.

On another note, it was only when I awoke the next morning that I realized that I had forgotten about my plan for a girl-talk session.

I, Larna Smith, also known as Susanna Randall, had made my way up to the roof of a building a little removed from the inn we were staying over at tonight.

The roof of this building was easily the tallest point in the surrounding areas. Of course, I got permission from the homeowner to go up here. While I could climb up regardless of permissions, behavior like that could cause issues down the road.

The reason I was currently in such a tall place to begin with was because of the nature of the magical tool I was about to use. I withdrew it from my bag and held it up to the sky. It didn't take long before it started vibrating. "Good." This meant that it was working correctly.

I turned to it and started to speak. "Hello? This is Larna Smith. Are you receiving, Raphael Wolt?"

"Ah, yes. I hear you clearly, Lady Larna." The somewhat displeased voice of my subordinate rang out from the tool.

"A success, I see." I grinned. This tool allowed us to speak over long distances. I had tested it and re-crafted it many times, and at long last, it was functional. Since the tool utilized Wind Magic, there were a few conditions that limited its use. Namely, I had to be outside and at a relatively high spot, which could be a challenge.

With more improvements, I may be able to put this tool into production... I suppose I'll have to make more modifications when I return.

"Lady Larna? Lady Larna, can you hear me?"

Just as I was about to sink deeper into my thoughts, Raphael's displeased voice dragged me back to reality.

"Ah, my apologies. I hear you, Raphael. Well? What of it? The situation back home."

"Don't 'what of it' me, Lady Larna... You can't just suddenly declare that you'd like to leave on a trip and push all your work onto me. Please give me a break..."

Ah, the pathetic voice of my subordinate. "But it won't be a problem for you, will it? Weren't you the top of your class back at the academy?" I said.

"But that..." He stopped short, seemingly embarrassed.

This wasn't just some excuse that I came up with; it was a true fact. Because of a certain incident last year, Raphael was in the protective custody of the Ministry. But due to the circumstances, not many in the Ministry were interested in taking him under their wing.

But I was interested in his yet-undiscovered potential, so I took him in. Since then, I've realized that he is a very capable person and that his abilities are quite useful. He is truly a valuable employee. *So... it's totally fine to leave all my work at the Ministry to him, for now.*

So I changed the subject, instead asking about a request I'd made. "Has there been any progress with regard to the investigation?"

Raphael eventually answered, albeit with a barely audible sigh. "...Yes. I have... managed some progress."

"As expected. Well then, what are we looking at?"

At my question, Raphael's voice took on a more serious tone. "Yes... well. Although Duke Claes himself has made quite a few moves, it would seem that there has yet to be any significant breakthroughs. No progress has been made by those in the Duke's employ... nor the Ministry at this point, really."

"I see. But to pull such a fast one on Duke Claes... This is no ordinary enemy. And what about the rumors that there was a Wielder of Darkness involved? Have we heard anything else?"

"That would be a more definitive thing to answer, Lady Larna. After all, there was an eyewitness who saw the magic itself being cast, so..."

"I see. So that much has been confirmed..."

It was a few weeks ago that rumors of another Wielder of Darkness had started to make the rounds. Honestly I was quite irritated at the news, since it meant that classified information had been leaked again. And then...

"Well then, are there any links between this Wielder of Darkness, and the disappearance of Keith Claes?"

"On that, we still do not know."

"I see..." When those two reports had landed on my desk, I couldn't help but feel that the two incidents were connected somehow. The sudden disappearance of Katarina's adopted brother, Keith, and the emergence of yet another Wielder of Darkness. They had to be connected. It was with this hunch that I had Raphael investigate.

"Ah, right. Do send a request under my name to Prince Jeffrey. I would like him to issue some investigative warrants and the like."

"Prince... Jeffrey, Lady Larna?" Raphael asked, confused.

"Yes. He owes me a few favors, you see, and I'm calling them in. Also, if the prince refuses to cooperate, then let him know that he won't be receiving a certain magical tool. Tell him that."

"...Right. Of course." Although Raphael seemed somewhat hesitant, he soon agreed without asking too many questions. For a while there was silence, and then he spoke once more. "If I may... how is Katarina doing?" he asked, the worry evident in his voice. Come to think of it, he was one of the many people who had a deep affection for Katarina Claes.

"Should I tell you not to worry, or should I let you worry regardless? Katarina seems to think that Keith's disappearance is the result of him running away from home. She also believes that all she has to do is find him, apologize, and he'll come back. After coming to terms with the situation in that way, she cheered up again, and now she's acting just like usual."

"Is that so... It is good that Katarina is doing well, then."

"Maria seems to believe in the runaway theory too. We should fear the pure souls of those girls. Sora and Prince Jeord, however... the two of them have surely already noticed that something is wrong, though neither has said anything directly."

"I see... However, if it would seem like someone is close to telling her outright... would an explanation not be better, then?"

"I suppose. If that happens, then I'll make sure everything is explained. But everything until now has played out like I thought it would. I'll be investigating on my end, so make sure you look into what we discussed as well."

"I understand."

"I'm counting on you, top-class Raphael." As I moved to end the conversation, I felt like I heard a sigh and "Really..." from the other end. Despite his reluctance, I knew he would conduct his investigations responsibly.

With that, I started making my way back to the inn. Katarina was there, sleeping soundly while believing that all Keith had done was run away from home. She would never think that he may have been kidnapped, or that his kidnapper may be a Wielder of Darkness. That would never occur to her, not in her wildest dreams. She probably didn't realize that the real reason why Maria and Sora, Wielders of Light and Darkness, were coming with us was because of this danger. Looking at the pure and kind Katarina, I, too, almost believed that Keith had run away from home.

Even Duke Claes and Madam Claes were in on this — they desperately announced their search for Keith, so as not to alarm Katarina with the possibility that he may have been kidnapped.

"…Please be safe, Keith Claes… for the sake of your pure and innocent sister," I said to no one in particular as I looked up at the night sky, slowly retracing my steps to the inn.

★★★★★★

My awakening at the inn was really nice. Normally Anne would be hissing at me right now, something like *What time do you intend to sleep until, young miss?!* But this time, it was Maria's voice that woke me up.

"Lady Katarina… if you do not wake up soon, we will really be late."

Waking up to her gentle voice was very different. But we were pressed for time, so I had to wake up and get ready as fast as possible. With Maria's help, I made it in time.

I didn't know when Larna had come back from wherever she went, but she was already fully dressed when I awoke, and was elegantly drinking some black tea as she waited. Jeord was the same, maybe because he was a prince. He was already dressed, groomed, and waiting for me in a tidy outfit. The two of them greeted me with kind smiles, disregarding the fact that I'd come so late.

The only one who didn't seem happy to see me was Ugly Bear, which was currently sitting next to Larna. It looked up at me and shot a glance that seemed to say *"Hmph. You useless bum."* Not to be outdone, I returned the look with a mental insult of *"Oh look, it's Bratty Bear."*

Sora wasn't here, and I assumed he'd overslept even more than I did — only to find out that he had set off into town earlier, apparently to gather more information on Keith. He was really good at what he did!

Unfortunately, he hadn't found out anything important, and so it was time to keep going. Since we still hadn't found any information about Keith, I started to wonder if the bear was even leading us in the right direction. But Larna strongly insisted that it was accurate, so I had no choice but to believe her.

And so we all piled into the carriage again and set off for the next town. Ugly Bear, having become smitten with Maria yesterday, was sitting on her knees again and was currently being patted on the head. Although it normally had a cute and lovable expression, it would always scowl mockingly at me whenever our eyes met. This thing was really rude. There was no other way to put it.

Although our journey was pretty uneventful, I could feel my dislike of the bear intensifying, and vice versa. I knew it was childish to get upset at a stuffed toy... but that bear's attitude! Ugh! I couldn't do anything about the way it was acting, so of course I'd hate it.

The carriage rolled along, and not much happened. Although we asked about Keith at every place our carriage stopped, we didn't have any results. So we kept going, and before long, the sun had set.

It had now been two days since we'd set off. As the last of the sun's rays faded, we reached yet another town and decided to stop there for the night. It was rural and small compared to the one we'd stopped at the day before — there was no marketplace of any kind and the roads weren't paved. In fact, weeds were growing freely in every direction.

The carriage was parked at a location that was somewhat far from the inn, so we had to walk a bit to get there. If we were in a bigger town, we would have been flanked by shops of all kinds right now. But now there was nothing but weeds and shrubbery around us, so I just looked at the grass as we went. My eyes soon found a nostalgic sight.

"Ah, this seed!" I exclaimed, stopping in my tracks.

Maria, who had been walking next to me, asked inquisitively, "What is that, Lady Katarina?"

I held up a stickseed and showed it to Maria. I hadn't seen one in a long time. "It's a kind of seed that sticks to you if you brush against it! Haven't you seen one before?" I asked.

"No, this is the first time I've seen one," Maria replied.

Come to think of it, this was the first time I had seen stickseed plants in this life. Maybe this plant didn't grow in the region we lived in. In my previous life, tons of these seeds ended up stuck to my clothing every time I romped around the mountains, and my mom would always get angry at me. *Ah, how nostalgic.*

I gave Maria a demonstration, sticking a seed to my blouse. "You see? It sticks really well, right?"

"Oh! You're right!" Maria replied, her lovely face painted with surprise. "Whatever is it called?"

Although I almost blurted out "stickseed" in response, I stopped myself. After all, stickseed was what we called it... I didn't know the plant's scientific name. What was it called, actually...?

"Ah... Hmm. Sorry, I have absolutely no idea." Considering that I had made such a fuss about the plant in the first place, it was a little pathetic that I didn't even know its name.

"Ah, I see... I wonder what it is called, hmm?" Maria responded. Being the angel she was, she would never ridicule someone for something like this.

However... Ugly Bear, which had been riding on Maria's shoulders all this time after getting so familiar with her yesterday, evidently did not share her sentiment. *So you don't even know what the thing is called? Then don't bring it up, you hopeless fool.* That was what the bear's face seemed to be saying. Considering how bad our relationship was, I found it mysterious that I was understanding more and more of what that bear was thinking. It annoyed me.

That damn bear! As I tightened my grip around the stickseed in my hands, an idea suddenly leapt into my mind. *Heh... just you watch, bear...* I thought as a villainous smile crept onto my face.

When we reached the inn, we all tucked into our meals. Although the rural cooking had a delicious, rustic taste to it, I learned from my experiences yesterday and stopped myself from overeating.

We went to our rooms after we ate, and Larna left once again. I'd assumed she had been doing some night-time sightseeing yesterday; apparently, she had some Ministry-related work to take care of. She really was such a busy person.

So Maria and I went to our room and started talking about the towns we'd seen today, things that had happened back at the academy, and other silly things. After a while, Maria left to go to the washroom.

This was the chance I'd been waiting for. I slowly withdrew the stickseeds I had brought in my bag. Then, without warning, I threw them all at that annoying Ugly Bear as it sat haughtily on Maria's bed. As expected, the bear was now covered from head to toe in the spiky seeds.

Hahaha! How's that, you arrogant bear! Do you fear me now? Do you fear me?! You're nothing but a plush toy! This is what you get for messing with Katarina Claes, villainess extraordinaire. Upon affirming that my plan was a resounding success, I raised a hand to my lips, before bursting out in my trademark villainess laugh.

As for the bear... it had no idea what hit it. For a while it seemed stunned, but it soon grasped the situation. It tried to remove the stickseeds with its stubby arms, all the while glaring daggers at me. But it didn't have much luck. I continued treating it to a rendition of my best villainess laugh up until Maria's return.

When she saw the stickseed-riddled bear, Maria looked surprised. "Whatever has happened to the bear, Lady Katarina?" she asked.

"Oh, it... tripped and fell into some stickseeds," I replied.

The pure and innocent Maria immediately believed my words. My conscience hurt a little, yes, but it was impossible to tell her that I was simply serving Ugly Bear its just desserts.

In the end, the bear finally rid itself of the stickseeds with the gentle Maria's assistance. After that, the bear continued to glare at me when she wasn't looking. But justice had been served!

I was elated as I lay down to sleep. As I slipped under the sheets, I thought about how fond I was of stickseeds, and how I had given that bear its comeuppance with them today. *I'll tell Keith all about it,* I thought.

I would always tell Keith about everything that had happened that day between dinner and bedtime. In fact, ever since he'd come to live with our family, we had never been apart. Not like this.

Ah… I really want to see Keith again soon.

I'll make sure to apologize, so please come back and listen, Keith. I have so, so many things to tell you…

I was in a warm, sunny spot under the biggest tree at Claes Manor. I had fallen asleep immediately after lying down, tired out by all the fishing and dashing about.

Although I had fallen asleep in such a comfortable place, the dreams I had were of days long gone. Back when I was trapped in a narrow, dark place… When I was subjected to violence. That was what I remembered.

Now, things were different. My family loved and cherished me. I was happy now — impossibly happy, more so than I could have ever imagined. Each and every day was blissful. And yet, dreams of the past would haunt me occasionally, like they did now. It was as if the nightmares were telling me that my life now was nothing but a lie. That I was still cowering, shivering in that tiny room, all alone…

However, I was soon roused from those dreams. As I opened my eyes, I could see a girl standing over me with a worried expression. "Keith… are you okay?" Backlit by the glittering rays of the sun, that girl seemed to be a goddess, like the ones I had read about in books.

"…I'm okay, Big Sister. I just had a scary dream."

"Oh… you were talking and tossing, so I was worried. A scary dream, huh… I guess I should have woken you even earlier! I'm sorry, Keith!"

"It's alright… I apologize for worrying you," I replied.

"Hmm. But see, next time it'll be different! If it ever seems like you're having another scary dream, I'll wake you up right away, Keith!"

With that, Katarina puffed her chest out, as if to say *"Ha! Leave it all to me!"*

I opened my eyes… and Katarina was not there.

Ah… it was a dream. A dream of the past. A nostalgic, happy dream.

I often used to have nightmares about the past when I first moved to Claes Manor. Whenever I had those dreams, Katarina, who was very into playing the part of an elder sister back then, would always take care of me.

"I'll wake you, Keith! I'll hold your hand," she'd say. The girl I liked was saying things like *"I'll hold your hand until you fall asleep!"* and *"I'll go to sleep with you tonight!"* I was glad, but at the same time felt somewhat pathetic. It was a complicated series of emotions.

Eventually, I stopped having those nightmares. The days I spent with Katarina were so vibrant and refreshing. Full of bliss and joy. It didn't take me long at all to forget all about those dreams. In fact, it has been quite a while since I had recalled anything like this… was it due to the situation I was currently in? Wherein I am bound, my arms and legs restrained in a lightless room.

My mother, the very same woman who had discarded me before, had called out to me. Before I knew it, I was handed over to men I had never seen before and dragged here against my will.

Shortly after, I had my first reunion in years with my older brother, who was born to a different mother. He, Thomas, had been hitting me ever since. I suppose such a situation would indeed make me recall those dreams from so long ago. After all, I was currently being treated in a way that my old self was used to.

...Just how much time has passed? My family... Katarina is surely worried. That loving, warm, and gentle family I had come to first know at the age of eight... and the person I loved. My thoughts floated toward those people — people who had given me everything I could possibly want, and their magnanimity, their generosity. All this time, I had only received. I had yet to repay their kindness.

Although I was restrained and made to lie here, simple food was given to me at certain times. I couldn't tell if it was breakfast or dinner, though. So... I supposed that I wasn't going to die anytime soon. As for what would happen from here on out, as for what Thomas would do to me... I had no idea. But I could not simply die in a place like this. I still had many things to do. I still had to repay those who had been kind to me... and I wanted to be by Katarina's side.

That was why I did what I could to eat the crude food I was given... struggling like a restrained dog. All so that I would survive. The dark room and cold bed brought forth memories of the abuse I had endured in my childhood... but I could dispel them by thinking of Katarina. Her smile, as bright as the sun. Her warm hands, reaching out to me. Merely recalling them filled me with strength.

Although Thomas would pay me many visits, and proceed to perform acts of violence against me while I was powerless to fight back... I simply thought of Katarina, and passed the time. I would surely break free of this place and return to her side.

Those thoughts were what kept me going — thoughts of Katarina were the source of my strength.

It was slightly after Thomas had paid me yet another visit to hurl verbal abuse at me that the only door to the room opened again. I simply assumed that he had come back. Other than the wordless, sullen man who would bring me my food, Thomas was the only person who entered this room. As for the woman I had seen when I'd first awoken, I hadn't seen her since.

However, the one who entered the room now was the woman in question. She had that same innocent smile on her face as she entered. She stood before me, lowering herself to my height.

"How are you doing?" she asked, in a tone like she was talking about something inconsequential, like the weather.

I didn't know what this woman wanted, so I held my tongue and stared at her silently in response.

"Well, if you can look so focused, I suppose you're doing relatively well, huh?" She laughed.

Just like when I had first seen her, I felt like something about this woman was off. Although her appearance suggested that we weren't too far apart in terms of age, she was strangely childlike. There was also an aura of danger about her that I couldn't quite figure out. I found myself fearing her more than Thomas, even though the latter would always commit acts of violence against me. I held my peace, observing her.

She merely laughed at my response. "Haha. So you've been trapped here for a few days, bound, and continuously beaten... normally you'd become a little crazy, hm? As expected of the heir to the Claes family. Or is it simply because you got used to this during your childhood?"

From those words alone, it became clear to me that this woman knew about my past, and about everything I had done up until this point. "...What is your goal?" I asked.

"Haha! That, you see... I'd like you to... fall."

"...Fall? What... does that mean?"

"Oh, it means what it means, of course. I would like you to fall from your current position. From being the lofty heir of a Duke... all the way to the bottom. From your rarefied heights, to the abyss, you see."

"Height... to the abyss?" I had merely assumed that they had kidnapped me for a ransom of coin. I could not understand the words that spouted forth from her lips, and could only look on in surprise.

The woman merely laughed at me again. "Such was the wish that Thomas has made of me, you see. But then..." The woman pulled a troubled face as she continued. It was all fake, of course. "Thomas can't wait any longer, hm? He can't stand those straightforward eyes of yours! That unflinching gaze no matter how much pain he subjects you to." A smile crept across her features once more. "So... Keith Claes. I have decided that you shall become a guinea pig for my experiments."

"...Guinea... pig?" I felt a shiver travel down my spine. It was an unsettling phrase.

"Yes, a guinea pig for my experiments in the Dark Arts, you see. It's an experiment I have always wanted to try, but it requires an experimental subject with quite a strong will, you know? Even so, a single experiment is all it takes to break them, so I was in quite the bind... until Thomas said that he'd like to break you. What a serendipitous event, I thought, and so..."

"Experiment in the Dark Arts...? Break...?" Those words were said so innocently, as if the woman didn't harbor any malice. What she said didn't feel real. I could only stare blankly at her.

"I say break, but your body will remain as it is, you see. The only thing that we'll be breaking is your heart! That pretty body of yours will stay in one good piece. So don't you worry about it one bit," the woman said, smiling as she did so. "Well then… I suppose we might as well start soon, hm?"

At her words I finally moved my head, willing myself out of my stunned silence. *It'll be dangerous if I remain here,* I thought. I tried my best to move… but my body wouldn't budge.

In fact, I couldn't even make a sound — no words escaped my throat. I could only open my mouth and gape. I couldn't even close my eyes. All I could do was look at this woman before me, who was now chanting some sort of spell.

Before long, my field of vision was engulfed by darkness… before a heavier, denser darkness fell onto my entire being altogether.

"Fight and resist lots, okay? After all, that's how you get stronger creations…" The woman's innocent voice echoed sonorously in the darkness.

I screamed wordlessly, silently, the name of the person I loved most in the world.

Katarina…!

"Ah!"

As I heard what sounded like a cry of agony, I flew out of my bed.

Sunlight was already flooding in through the windows. For an instant, I panicked. This was a strange place that I didn't recognize! But I quickly recognized it as the inn we had stopped at for the night yesterday. In the other beds of the room, Maria and Larna were both still asleep.

I felt like I'd had a terrifying dream. I wiped away beads of sweat from my forehead. I felt like I couldn't fall back asleep, so I left the room.

Although it was still very early in the morning, the people who lived in this town were already up and about. I could hear their voices from outside the inn. The rural sights that greeted me as I looked out of a window reminded me of my home in my previous life.

As the nostalgia washed over me, I decided to step outside for a little bit, still dressed in my pajamas. The smell of the sun and the fields tickled my nose. I felt myself finally calming down a little, despite the terrifying dream I'd had. I stood for a while, looking out at the scenery.

"Katarina?" A voice called out to me from behind.

I turned around and saw that it was Jeord. The normally impeccably-dressed prince seemed like he wasn't entirely ready for the day — he looked a bit unkempt. But despite this, he exuded a unique, seductive aura. As expected of Prince Jeord.

"Good morning." Although I was dressed in my pajamas, I did my best to offer Jeord an elegant greeting… only for him to respond with a surprised expression.

"Katarina… what happened to your head?" he replied.

"Huh?" *What happened to my head?* Jeord smiled tensely as he slowly, hesitantly reached out to my head.

"These are stuck in your hair…" Jeord said, holding out something in his hand.

I peered at the object, only to find that it was none other than one of the stickseeds I'd found yesterday. *Huh?! Stickseed?* I ran my hands through my hair in a panic, only to find that the prickly seeds were indeed scattered all over my head.

85

Why would something like this...? I thought I remembered all of the seeds I'd found yesterday being stuck onto the bear. And then the bear was trying desperately to remove them...

"...Ah!" *That's right... what happened to the stickseeds that got stuck on that Ugly Bear, then?* Come to think of it, Maria did offer to throw the seeds away, only for the bear to respond with a gesture that seemed to suggest, *"Oh, I'll do it myself."* But I didn't remember seeing the bear toss the seeds away.

In other words... the stickseeds in my hair were most likely... the work of that Ugly Bear!! *Ugh! Just when I served it its just desserts, and it returned the favor!?*

I've been had! The bear strikes back! I've been too careless! I stomped the ground savagely in my rage. Jeord merely stood still, regarding me with a vague gaze as I clenched my teeth, stomping my foot at odd intervals.

My anger subsided after a while, and Jeord began to remove the stickseeds from my hair. I had tried to remove them myself, of course, but I couldn't see where the seeds were and I was never good at this sort of thing, so I couldn't quite get them off at all.

Jeord, on the other hand, always had an eye for detail and was quite dexterous with his fingers. His smooth, long fingers weaved through my hair, and soon all the seeds were gone. "There you go, Katarina. I have removed every last one," Jeord said, before patting me several times on the head.

"Thank you very much," I said, blushing for reasons unknown even to myself.

"You are most welcome, Katarina. On another note... whatever are you doing out here, at this time of the day?"

"Ah, yes. Well... I had a terrifying dream and woke up..."

"A terrifying dream, you say?"

"Yes. I don't really remember it very well… but it was really unsettling." Just recalling what little I could remember of the dream sent shivers down my spine. I folded my arms, holding myself reflexively.

Jeord's expression clouded as he saw this. "…As I thought. Of course you would be worried in some capacity."

"Hm?"

"While he is a most troublesome opponent in my eyes, he is an important member of your family to you, no doubt. Originally, I had planned to be a little more aggressive in my approach during this trip… but I suppose I should restrain myself."

"Um?" I didn't understand what he was talking about.

Upon witnessing my confusion, Jeord smiled at me, looking somewhat lonely. "And then there is that, too… you had finally noticed, and then you went and forgot all about it, it would seem. And so, Katarina… I suppose this is enough, for now."

Jeord suddenly reached out to me, pulling me in with both his arms. Before I knew it, he was hugging me tight. It was very surprising and sudden, yes, but I felt my shivering eventually cease as I was held in his strong, warm arms.

Ah, I see. He's trying to comfort me. He really is a gentle person at heart. In fact, I was surrounded by gentle and kind people. I really was blessed.

For a while, I remained in Jeord's embrace… only to be suddenly removed from it. *Hmm?* From what I could see, Jeord hadn't let go of me intentionally. I guess someone had pulled me away.

"Ah, good morning, Prince Jeord, Lady Katarina," said Sora, who was now suddenly standing next to me.

"…Sora. Surely you could overlook something like this, no?" Larna said, a somewhat pained expression on her face as she did so.

Sora merely grinned as he offered a response. "Merely doing my job."

"I feel like there is more to that, perhaps," Jeord said as his gaze swept over Sora.

But Sora's smile didn't falter as he said, "Nothing of the sort, Prince Jeord."

As usual, I had no idea what the two of them were going on about. But soon my shivers had gone away, and now... I was hungry.

Upon hearing the loud rumbling of my stomach, the two of them smiled wryly, and I headed back to my room.

When I came back, I changed my clothes and then headed for the dining area. I sat down for my breakfast, and after having my fill, promptly looked into the matter at hand — finding the culprit who had put the stickseeds in my hair. As expected, it was none other than Ugly Bear.

The bear had an excuse for this, claiming that it had accidentally spilled the seeds on me after gathering them into a pile. That was a lie, of course. For the record, the bear couldn't speak; it just gestured to explain the chain of events.

No one else knew about the bear's true nature, so they all believed it! As much as I wanted to, I couldn't just declare, *"It's a lie, a complete lie! It's obvious that the bear did it on purpose!"* After all, I had put the seeds on the bear with a similar lie to begin with.

In the end, the bear and I suffered equally. I was not happy at all about the situation, but there wasn't anything I could do about it now.

And so we all got in the carriage, bear included, and set off again. This was the third day of our journey. Larna soon pointed out that we would reach the kingdom's rural borders soon. If we kept going like this, we might end up entering the neighboring country's territory.

Honestly, I hadn't expected Keith to travel this far. It was surprising that he'd come all this way. Was Ugly Bear really right? Were we really following in his footsteps?

In this life, I had never set foot outside the kingdom where I was born, though it's not like I had in my previous life either. Japan was an island, after all. Anyway, the kingdom I'd been reincarnated into was large and developed, so I'd always stayed within its borders. Jeord and Alan were a different story. They had been on many diplomatic trips abroad, though usually the other kingdoms would come to us, given that our land was the largest.

If we kept our pace, I would soon leave this kingdom for the first time. Although they were foreign kingdoms, people there spoke the same language and had a similar culture, so it wouldn't be that different. And unlike in my previous life, we didn't need a passport or any documents like that. Even so, going abroad was still something new, and I was excited at the prospect. *I wonder what these foreign lands are like?*

We were two towns away from crossing the borders when Sora decided to go out on his own again to gather information.

"I'd like to go too!" I said in response. Up until now, I had been paired with Larna. From our previous conversation, it sounded like Sora's way of life was like a spy's, the kind of thing you'd see in the movies. I wanted to see it in action at least once.

But when I made my declaration, Jeord immediately said, "I shall accompany you, Katarina."

I see... Jeord wants to observe Sora's professional techniques up close as well, huh?

But Sora was quick to refuse. "In that case, Prince Jeord, please conduct your search in the opposite direction, if you would."

Only for Jeord to respond, "In that case, I shall accompany Katarina. Surely you alone would be sufficient to conduct a search in said direction."

"But you see, I am more used to places such as this, and as such, Lady Katarina would be more safe with me."

"Is that so? I, however, cannot help but feel that you yourself carry a sense of danger."

"Surely you jest, Prince Jeord. I am at least more of a gentleman than you are."

"I am thoroughly surprised that you would make such a claim. After all, I have already heard from Katarina the... specifics, of your actions during that incident."

Larna, seemingly oblivious to the atmosphere between those two, soon intervened in their conversation (which I didn't understand at all). "I'm not exactly clear on what you two are talking about, but it's a waste of time to stand around talking. As Sora says, he is more used to places like this, so Katarina should stay with him on this excursion." And with that, Larna sealed the deal, without waiting for input from anyone in particular.

Jeord seemed displeased about this right until the end. "You really do understand, yes? I am Katarina's rightful fiancé," he said to Sora. Then he turned to me. "Do be careful from here on out, Katarina," he said, and then repeated it several times.

It was all a little too much for me. "I get it, I understand! I won't get in the way of his questioning, or his work! I won't become lost either!" I said, puffing out my chest as I did so. Jeord, for some reason, merely responded with a faraway gaze. I wonder why?

And so Sora and I set off for the small town in hope of finding some information on Keith. Maybe it was because we were a lot closer to the border, but the general feel of the town we were in was very different from the last one. Since it was so small, there weren't many shops. But there were all kinds of plants that I'd never seen before. My eyes wandered over the foreign elements of the architecture of the buildings around us. I was ogling at my surroundings without even realizing it.

When he noticed this, a mild smile flitted across Sora's face. "Is all this new to you?"

"Yes, everything is new to me! Each of the towns we've been to up until now has had something new, and this one has all kinds of things I've never seen before. After all, I've never been outside the capital before, so a trip like this is really different for me."

"Come to think of it, you did mention somethin' like that." Sora started laughing softly.

"What is it?" I asked.

"Ah, well see, I just never thought we'd actually go on a trip like this, you know?" Sora had reverted back to his normal way of speaking.

Now that he mentioned it, I remembered listening to Sora's stories about his experiences abroad during that time I spent with him. And now it had become a reality, and so soon!

"We live in different worlds, I thought. Thought we could never be together like this, heh." Just like he had said back then! And I responded the same way I had before.

"What are you talking about? We're here in the very same world, you and I."

"Yeah. Here we are, taking a trip like this together after all. And this is thanks to you, too." Sora withdrew a familiar-looking object from his pocket. It was the blue gemstone brooch that I had given him before.

"Wow! You held on to it all this time…" It was just a souvenir I'd bought during the school festival, and the brooch wasn't worth very much, of course. But it made me happy that he was holding on to it like that.

"Of course I did. It's a special stone, right? The color of your eyes and mine. I'll treasure it forever." Sora smiled at me — an innocent smile, like the one I saw back then. Compared to the refined smile he'd had plastered on his face during this whole trip, this suited him much better.

"Haha, you see Sora, this smile suits you a lot better than that polite one you've had on your face all this time!" I said.

Sora froze in response, smile and all, and then suddenly took me into his arms.

"Hm?" *Huh? What's this all of a sudden? A hug? Hmm. Come to think of it, something similar happened before.*

Hmm… could it be? Sora is foreign, after all. Is this some sort of foreign greeting?

Sora merely smiled at me again as I stood, rooted to the ground. His smile was a little more reserved this time, though. "You really are something, huh? How do you have such a knack for reeling in the guys, left and right…"

Reeling in? Hmm? Reeling in… fish? How did we end up talking about fishing?

"…And you really don't have your guard up at all. It's no wonder Prince Jeord is so worried about you." With that, Sora released me from his hug. "Honestly, I'd like to keep whiling the time away with you like this… but it would be a pain if Prince Jeord found us, huh. Shall we go on with our questioning then, my lady?"

"Ah… okay." I didn't really understand how this conversation had turned out this way, but I suppose he'd meant it as a greeting, right? And what was all that about dumplings, again? *Well… I guess everything's fine.*

After that, we headed into the town, wandering about and searching for any information on the whereabouts of Keith.

Although we did make several rounds through the town, no information was to be found here either, as expected.

"Hmm… If there really is nothing here either, we might really enter foreign territories during our search…" I said, with just a little of my excitement showing.

"Aren't you having a little too much fun?" Sora replied, shooting me a surprised look.

Ugh… I've been found out! I decided to tell Sora up-front about my excitement about entering a foreign land.

But when he heard what I had to say, Sora's expression changed; he seemed troubled. "But… it's not all fun and games, you know."

"Why? After all, you told me so many interesting things when I was listening to your stories back then, right?" Back during the kidnapping incident, I had heard all kinds of stories from Sora about his adventures in foreign lands. As I had never been abroad before, I was swept up in it all. It made me want to take a little trip myself.

"It is true that foreign lands have all sorts of things this kingdom doesn't. Interesting things. But on the flip side, there's a lot of dangers too."

"Dangers…?" I couldn't imagine what kind of dangers he was talking about.

"Well ya see, the kingdom you were born in — the Kingdom of Sorcié — is known for its peace and order. There's a lot more crime in other lands."

"Oh? Really?" The area where I'd lived in my previous life was known for its peace and quiet too. It was a rural part of the country. *Did we have any crime there? Hm... Tanuki stealing from gardens, maybe?*

The Kingdom of Sorcié, where I'd been reincarnated, was that way too. I was lovingly raised in Claes Manor, and usually had servants with me when I went to towns outside the capital. So I had never come into contact with any devious crimes. Maybe that was why I never really thought much about safety.

When I said as much to Sora, he looked even more surprised. "Huh? But I used the Dark Arts on you, ya know? And I kidnapped you. That's a crime, right?" He started muttering under his breath to himself, but then regained his usual composure. "Well... I suppose we can chalk this up to your perceptions being completely out of whack..."

Huh? What's this about my perception, now?

"...Anyway, the surrounding lands can't hold a candle to Sorcié when it comes to things like law and order. Especially Le Sable, the nation we're closest to. It's known as a lawless hellhole. Certain things are outlawed on the surface, but the slave trade is huge there."

"...Slave trade..." Since I was raised in a peaceful environment, those were words I had only heard in books. It was a lot to take in, and for a while, I fell silent.

Sora seemed even more troubled. "It happens in all the other countries. In fact, it's very normal in the place I was born."

"..." Born and raised in peace, I had only heard the interesting tales about foreign lands, so I always thought they'd be interesting to visit. *I guess I don't know anything...* I felt ashamed. "...I wanted to rush in head-first without thinking... I feel like an idiot," I said, hanging my head.

"You really are honest, huh. But that's fine, see. If there's something you don't know, then all you have to do is to learn about it, right?"

"Learn if there's something I don't know… Yes. Yes, you're right." All I had to do was keep an open mind, and I'd learn about all these things that I'd never experienced before. Acting on that idea immediately, I decided to ask Sora about the nation of Le Sable, and also about Noir, the town that we were going to next.

"As I mentioned, Le Sable is infamous for being lawless. So criminals are really common there. I've heard the slave trade is huge there, and is a lot bigger than anywhere else nearby. Noir is a town that sits on Sorcié and Le Sable's border. Even though it's in Sorcié, Noir has a bad reputation when it comes to safety."

"Is… that so…" Even here, there was a place like that… I now felt a little afraid to go in that direction.

Hmm? Wha? But then… "…Would Keith really be in a place as dangerous as that? If he was going to run away to another country, wouldn't it make sense to choose a safer place…?" I didn't even have to think to know that Keith, who had such a good head on his shoulders, would never choose to run away to such a dangerous place.

"Guess that's true, yeah…" Sora muttered, once again with that troubled expression.

Is Keith really beyond this point? Does the bear really know what it's doing? I really want to find him soon. Is he really in such a dangerous place? And if he is, is he safe? What if something's happened to him? The shivers that had run down my spine before were suddenly back in full force. I felt a deep sense of unease.

After we were done questioning the locals, I returned to the carriage with Sora. Jeord immediately leapt out to greet us. "Did he do anything to you? Are you alright?"

Again with the strange questions... And why's he staring at my neck? Hmm? What?

In the end, there was no useful information to be found in this small town at all. With that in mind we set off once more, for the border town of Noir.

The sun was already setting by the time we arrived at Noir. Sora said that it wasn't a safe place at all, but this wasn't obvious at first glance. It seemed to me like a normal, busy town. But when I looked closer, I noticed that there were people around who gave me a bad vibe.

Apparently not just Sora knew this town well, but Larna and Jeord too. There was no unnecessary sight-seeing here — our group immediately went to an inn after we'd done some information-gathering. I made sure to do my part here, sticking with everyone else instead of wandering away aimlessly. I didn't stare at any storefronts either.

As our group continued our quiet advance, Maria suddenly came to a stop. *Hm? Is there a store she's interested in?* A quick look at her face, and I could tell from her grave expression that this wasn't the case. Everyone else noticed too, and soon the entire group stopped. For a while, she just stayed like that, not moving a single step.

Worried, I finally called out to her. "Maria... Maria! What's wrong?"

She gasped and suddenly turned to face me. "Ah, Lady Katarina... I just... for a moment there, I thought I saw..."

"Hmm? What did you see?"

"…Um… That is…" I waited for her to go on, and while hesitant, she eventually kept speaking. "I thought I saw someone over there… who was being dominated by the Dark Arts. But why would that be?" she whispered quietly. "Surely it must have been my imagination." She laughed haltingly.

As Maria said, after the previous events involving Dark Magic, there was a strict crackdown on it. Other than Sora, there really shouldn't have been anyone capable of using it around these parts. Even Sora wasn't allowed to use his magic without express permission of the Ministry. It was more than strange for Maria to feel the presence of Dark Magic here, so I could believe that it may have been just her imagination.

But Larna's expression completely changed when she heard this. "Where did you see it, Maria? An approximation is fine."

"Ah… no. It was just my imagi—"

"Whatever it may be, I want to know. Tell me." Larna's voice took on a severe tone — it was really intimidating, honestly.

Maria replied, somewhat stutteringly. "It was… the person who passed us just now. I couldn't see them clearly… they had a black hood on. I couldn't see their face. They walked past us and in that direction…"

"How intense was it? The Dark Arts presence."

"…Um. It was a bit like a wispy mist around that person's body. It wasn't strongly attached to them… but I felt a fear that… I have never felt until now…" Maria finished, her face pale.

A slight smile returned to Larna's face. "Thank you for telling us, Maria," she said, before quickly ushering us toward the inn we were stopping at today. Honestly, I had no idea what was going on. But Larna's strict expression made it feel like there was no room for negotiation. Our group quietly headed toward the inn in question.

The inn that we were stopping at today came highly recommended by Sora. Larna had looked into it too, and found that it was the safest place this town had to offer.

Although everyone wanted an explanation for Larna's reaction from earlier, she immediately left as soon as we checked in, saying that she had "matters to attend to."

Not sure what else to do, we all went to our rooms for the night. As before, our group was split into two rooms: one for the ladies, and another for the men. Larna had taken the bear with her as she left, so Maria and I found ourselves seated at a table in the room by ourselves.

Up until now, we had been talking eagerly about the new sights and sounds we came across each day. We had a lot to talk about normally, but the mood was different now. Few words were exchanged between us as we sipped our tea. Even the delicious treats in front of us that were apparently Noir's specialty were left mostly untouched. Normally I would have eaten nearly everything, but for some reason I couldn't bring myself to now.

Maria in particular didn't seem to be feeling well. She hadn't touched the treats. I tried to get her to eat something, but all she would say was "Perhaps later…"

"Maria? Are you okay?" I asked eventually. The color hadn't returned to her face, even after all this time.

"Yes… I'm alright," she replied in a weak, quavering voice that suggested that the opposite was true. Maybe she was still in shock from sensing the presence of Dark Magic. Even I couldn't help but feel an oppressive sense of fear just hearing that phrase.

I'd felt terrified when I first learned about the concept of Dark Magic. And yet I'd run into it not once, but twice since then. It was supposedly a huge national secret, according to Raphael and Jeord. I also remembered that someone who was strong in magic who gained the power of Dark Magic could easily crush someone's heart. It was really a terrifying thing.

Maria seemed badly shaken. The color of her face was abnormally pale. After all, she had experienced Dark Magic twice herself as well, and she had seen it both times. Since it could only be perceived by Wielders of Light, I had no idea what it looked like. It's possible that it looked horrifying.

Even so, I had never seen Maria this terrified before. *I wonder what happened? What did she see?* "Maria, why are you so afraid? Did you really see something that terrifying?" I asked, deciding to be straightforward about it. Maria hesitated for a few moments, not replying. "Isn't it better to talk about what's scaring you? You might feel a little better," I said.

"Perhaps you are right," she replied, trying her best to smile. She began to describe her experience. "How should I put this... It was different. Different than the Dark Magic I've seen up until now. It was disgusting, abnormal, horrifying, terrifying... I cannot quite get it out of my head," she said, shivering.

It really must have been awful. I couldn't stand to watch her sit there feeling that way. Before I knew it I'd moved close to Maria, and was soon holding her tight.

"Oh!" Maria's eyes opened wide in surprise.

"It'll be easier to calm down like this, right?" I said, giving her my warmest smile.

"...Yes, Lady Katarina," she whispered shyly.

When we were children, Keith would often bolt up in his sleep, his face pale from nightmares. I would always hold him like this, and soon color would return to his face. After that, I had even held Keith's hand when we went to sleep together.

Of course, I stopped doing that as we grew older, but I still remember those times as if it were yesterday. Since I was the youngest in my family in my previous life, I was really happy to have my little brother rely on me like that. It made me feel like a true big sister. Of course, then Keith became good at everything and perfectly able to take care of himself shortly after that...

There was Dark Magic in this town. Not just any Dark Magic, but powers strong enough to terrify Maria. Someone in this town was capable of that. And then... there was the possibility that Keith was even farther away.

As I held the shivering, terrified Maria, memories of my brother crying as a child floated through my mind. *Hey, Keith... You're okay, right? You're not... crying somewhere, right?*

★★★★★★

I, Larna Smith, with my magical tool Alexander in tow, once again found myself standing on the roof of the tallest building in this town in order to contact my subordinate, Raphael. This building was unfortunately home to some unpleasant-looking men; criminals, probably.

"Please let me use your roof for a little while," I had asked politely. But they weren't the kind of people who could be reasoned with. Without any other choice, I used some magic to encourage the louts to exit the premises. As a result, the building was now completely deserted and quiet, perfect for receiving transmissions.

I raised the transmitter to the night sky once more, and called out to my employee. "This is Larna Smith. Can you hear me, Raphael?"

"Yes. This is Raphael Wolt. I hear you loud and clear."

Upon confirming that Raphael could hear me, I explained what Maria had witnessed earlier. It would seem that there was someone in this town who could use the Dark Arts.

Raphael spoke up after I finished my explanation. "Actually, we received some new information on our end too, and I was planning on reporting it to you today." He continued, somewhat stiffly, "With regard to the information obtained from Prince Jeffrey... the individual who was seen making contact with Keith Claes on the day of his disappearance has been identified."

"Is that so? Well then, who is it?"

"Well, it appears to be Keith's biological mother."

"His actual mother? The ex-prostitute, right?"

"Yes, the very same. It would seem that his birth mother approached him as he was walking out of the downtown district. There was a witness who happened to see the whole thing. His description of Keith matched his appearance, and his mother was... somewhat memorable, so..."

"Are you telling me that Keith left with his mother, then?"

"No, it seems that his mother's role was simply to lure him into a trap, in exchange for a sum of coin. Someone paid her to entrap her son." Raphael's voice became more severe as the conversation went on. I supposed he was angry at how Keith's birth mother had so easily handed her son over to strangers in exchange for gold. After all, Raphael's mother loved him dearly, from the bottom of her heart. Maybe he couldn't bring himself to believe that mothers such as Keith's could even exist in this world.

I, however, knew that parents like that did exist. After all, I was born into noble society. There were many parents in this world who treated their children as nothing more than objects.

"Well then, did we find this person who Keith was handed over to?"

"The mother apparently has no memory of the incident."

"No memory? Isn't she just lying?"

"Yes, that was what I thought too, at first. But after some questioning, it became apparent that she really does not remember. As I continued to question Keith's mother, I observed her, and she displayed signs that Dark Magic had been cast on her. And that was…"

"…I see. As I thought — a Wielder of Darkness is involved in this entire chain of events…" I said, sighing.

"That would appear to be the case, Lady Larna," he replied, a hard edge to his voice.

"In that case, the person Maria spotted just now has a high possibility of being involved with Keith's disappearance. In any case, I'll use Alexander and attempt to pinpoint his exact location. It might even be possible that Keith may be in this very town."

"Please do be careful. If we receive any new information on our end, I will be sure to contact you."

"I understand. I'm counting on you, top-class Raphael." Immediately after terminating the transmission, I tasked Alexander with the job.

Now that it had come to this, it was no longer possible to hide these events from Katarina and the rest. If Keith's location could be pinpointed, I'd have to tell them everything. *I really don't want to worry Katarina, but… this is too serious now.* Steeling my resolve, I began walking in the direction Alexander had pointed out.

Larna hadn't still come back by evening, and I was worried about her. She eventually came back well after sunset, with an impossibly grave expression on her face.

I was worried when Larna didn't return until late into the night, but she eventually came back just as the day was about to end. Her expression was impossibly grave.

Without wasting any time, Larna gathered everyone into our room. "There is something I must tell all of you," she said, looking more serious than I'd ever seen her. "We went out to search for the runaway Keith... but it turns out, he did not run away from home."

I swallowed hard. *Keith... didn't run away? What happened then?*

"From the beginning, the Ministry was tasked with an official request from Duke Claes to investigate the matter. The result of that investigation has now revealed that Keith's disappearance was in fact... a kidnapping."

"A kidnapping!!" I stood up, shouting in surprise. *So Keith didn't run away from home... He was kidnapped?!*

"Yes. Keith Claes has been kidnapped."

Larna's words hit me like a waterfall. It was as if I'd been plunged into a sea of ice-cold water. I had never been this shocked and terrified in my life.

From what we were told, Keith had met with his birth mother, who he hadn't seen for many years, on the day he'd disappeared. He was led somewhere, and then handed over to someone else.

They had just found out about the most shocking development yet: Keith's mother had been a victim of the Dark Arts. She couldn't remember who had asked her to lure him into a trap, and she couldn't remember who she handed him over to, either.

The truth was a little too much for me. All I could do was gape wordlessly as Larna continued her explanation. I had thought, all the way until now, that Keith had run away from home because of the trouble I'd caused him. I thought that all we needed to do was find him, I would apologize, and he'd come right back home. But a kidnapping? Dark Magic? I couldn't wrap my mind around it.

Jeord, who had been standing next to me all this time, was the first to speak. He also looked very grave. "In the end, were we able to verify the identity of the individual who used that Dark Magic in the first place?" Unlike me, Jeord was always on top of things. He already seemed to understand the entire situation.

"...No, not yet. The enemy has been eluding us. We haven't been left a trace," Larna said, her expression twisting in vexation.

The cogs in my head finally started grinding into gear. In other words, Keith had been kidnapped, but we still didn't know who the culprit was.

"Then where is Keith now? Do we not know anything?" I asked.

Larna paused, falling silent for a while as she seemed to be thinking. Then she spoke with measured, heavy words. "...No. It's not that we don't know anything. There is at least a place that I have my eye on. I think he may be there."

"Wh-Wha?! Where is it? Where is he?" I leaned forward.

"After everyone settled down here, I used Alexander a little more to look into his whereabouts," Larna explained. "You all remember how Maria mentioned that she'd seen someone who was being influenced by Dark Magic, right? This incident also has ties to a Wielder of Darkness. Although the existence of Dark Magic has been kept under wraps, it's a given that there's been some leaks here and there. It may be wishful thinking, but the fact that a magical tool brought us here to find Keith and that we crossed paths with someone being controlled by Dark Magic doesn't seem like a coincidence."

Then she continued, "Also, Maria can only see traces of Dark Magic that have been performed recently. So it's logical to conclude that Keith is somewhere in this town. So with that in mind, I conducted my search."

"Well... did you find him?"

"Yes, actually. Alexander pointed out, relatively clearly, a certain mansion in the area."

Upon hearing those words, I immediately stood up from my chair once more. "Please tell me where it is. I'll go! I'll go right now!" *I'll come save you right away, Keith!*

Jeord's hands went to my shoulders, and soon I was gently but firmly seated back in my chair. "At this time of night? It is too dangerous. In any case, you would do well to calm down before deciding what to do." He grabbed a nearby sweet and quickly deposited it into my mouth.

As I started chewing in response, Jeord, who had been standing next to me this entire time, turned toward Larna. "I understand your words well, Lady Larna. I do apologize for saying this, but this is the first time that magical tool of yours has been used in the field, yes? Have there been any other, more concrete reports that would affirm the accuracy of this information? That this is indeed the place?" he asked bluntly.

The bear, sitting next to Larna, looked displeased. But Larna's expression didn't falter. "It is as you say. This tool is merely at the prototyping stage. It would be difficult to say with absolute certainty that Keith Claes is in this mansion with the aid of this tool alone. However, we may be able to confirm whether there is a presence of Dark Magic in or around the mansion. Since we know that Dark

Magic was involved in the kidnapping, it would solidify our lead if we discovered that there were signs of it around the mansion."

"The presence of Dark Magic... Do you mean to have Maria appraise this mansion?"

"Exactly. Though we won't only be using Maria's skills, but Sora's as well. We should be able to glean some knowledge through both their sets of eyes."

"...Lady Larna. Did you know of this all along? Was that why you had these two specific people accompany us?"

"Ha. You give me too much credit, Prince Jeord. I merely had the two of them with me just in case."

Nom nom nom. As Larna and Jeord had yet another difficult to understand, yet seemingly meaningful conversation, I finally finished the snack Jeord had stuffed into my mouth. But I was listening while I was chewing! Maria and Sora would look at the manor where Keith might be, and then we'd know how to proceed from there.

"Okay then, let's go right now," I said, standing up again.

But Larna quickly stopped me. "We should wait for daybreak. The mansion is somewhat far from the town of Noir. It's practically on the outskirts."

And so Larna convinced me to wait, and we soon returned to our rooms for some rest. Honestly though, even though I knew I should, I didn't think I'd be able to fall asleep. After all, Keith had been kidnapped... possibly by a Wielder of Darkness. I had no idea what kind of danger he might be in.

All I could think about was Keith. Even after I curled up in bed, I couldn't fall asleep. This was the first time that had ever happened; even when I myself was kidnapped, I had fallen asleep easily.

Eventually the tiredness from the day of travel caught up with me, and I found myself drifting away. And then, I had a dream.

A boy was hugging his knees and crying. With his flaxen hair, he looked exactly like Keith when he had been little. He was crying with such sorrow, it was too sad to watch. I tried my best, everything I could, to comfort him. But it was like he couldn't hear a single word I said. I would try to reach out and hug him, but I couldn't touch him, even if I reached out.

There was nothing I could do. All I could do was stand and watch as the boy continued to cry.

As the sun rose, and I woke from my shallow sleep and realized that my cheeks were wet. It must have been because of that terrible dream.

Under normal circumstances, I would forget about dreams like that right away... but I resolved to engrave that dream into my memory, so that I would never forget.

I had realized that the boy in my dream was Keith... and my heart ached.

The sun had risen. Normally the breakfast table was full of lively and cheerful conversations, but today a tense aura hung in the air, and everyone ate their food in silence.

Soon enough, we all finished our preparations. We headed to the area pointed out to us by the bear — the place we were told of yesterday that supposedly held Keith. Although the location was in the same town of Noir, it was somewhat far away from our inn. We boarded our carriage, but planned to disembark when we were halfway there and travel the rest of the way on foot.

This was natural. If we went with an entire horse-drawn carriage, the perpetrators would definitely notice us. For some reason, we were also using a different carriage than the one we'd arrived in yesterday; this one was a lot more beaten up. Maybe this was also to deceive our foes. But I learned later that this wasn't the only reason.

"How... How horrible..." I muttered. It was the only response I could think of as I looked at the scenes outside through the carriage's window as it rumbled along.

Larna raised her eyebrows slightly and turned to me. "This part of town has always been lawless. Honestly, places like this should have been cleaned up a long time ago. But geographical influences on its culture are strong, since it's so close to a foreign nation. Try as we might, the security around these parts has stubbornly refused to improve."

Staring out of the small window, I saw people dressed in filthy clothing sleeping by the side of the road, next to mountains of rubbish. These people were so dirty that it made them hard just to look at, and some of them were also terribly thin.

"If we had gone through here with that borrowed merchant's carriage of ours, we would have stood out too much. Don't look outside too much, Katarina. They don't let you go once your eyes meet."

Taking Larna's advice, I peeled my eyes away from the window. It felt real to me now — the fact that this was a lawless, dangerous place.

We eventually reached a point where the carriage, shabby as it was, would still stand out too much. Larna gave me a cloak of some kind to wear as we got off, and I obediently put it on. The fabric was dirty and thin, but wearing it was necessary to blend in. The clothing we were normally wearing would have drawn attention to us.

And so the five of us, all dressed in dirty hooded cloaks, grouped up and were led by Larna toward our destination. I was told that I should never meet the eyes of any of the people sleeping on the street, and that I should never turn around. All I could do was stare blankly ahead as I walked silently. It was a suffocating feeling.

"I can see the place now," Larna said about ten minutes after we'd started walking.

I looked up ahead of us. In the distance stood a grand mansion that stuck out like a sore thumb around its filthy surroundings.

"…That place?" It was so big that, as we approached it, it became harder to look at the entire building. It really didn't suit its surroundings at all. It was too extravagant, and too quiet. "Why is there a mansion like that in a place like this?" I muttered, confused by the contrast.

"It's the mansion of whoever rules over this area, I suppose. I can't imagine that any respectable person would be living in a place like this. Take a look, the security is tight."

I looked where Larna had pointed. Sure enough, there were a few bulky, muscular men positioned around the place, keeping a sharp eye on their surroundings. As I looked around more, I saw that there were a lot of them positioned around the mansion. It made sense that a fancy house in such a crime-ridden place had to have some type of security, but this was a bit much; it was overflowing with guards. There was no way we could approach easily.

"Last night, I knew I couldn't get any closer without causing a scene," Larna said, turning toward everyone and then addressing Maria and Sora. "But if you two can't get a good idea of the situation from here, I could cause a distraction so that you can. What do you think?"

Maria shook her head. "No, that is quite alright. This will do."

"Can you see anything, then? Or should we…"

"I see it. It is the same presence as the one I saw yesterday."

With Maria's confirmation, the party collectively tensed. Larna turned to Sora. "Do you see it too, Sora?" she asked.

"Well… not as well as Lady Maria, no. But I can sense that something is lurking there." Apparently Sora, being a Wielder of Darkness, could feel what Maria had too. So there was no doubt about it. This was the place.

"Then Keith is in there! We have to save him, quickly!" I said, ready to dash into the mansion.

Jeord quickly restrained me. "It would be impossible to run head-first into such a heavily-guarded mansion, Katarina. Take a moment to calm yourself," he said strictly. There was a hint of anger in his voice.

I guess he's right... I thought as I calmed down. "...Yes. Sorry..."

Seeing that I had changed my mind, Jeord nodded. "Alright then." He was definitely acting as my guardian at this point. "But yes, I see now that there is a high possibility of Keith being held in this place. What shall we do, Lady Larna? Break in?"

Larna placed a hand under her chin, deep in thought.

"U-Um..." Maria interjected, stuttering.

"What is it, Maria? You don't look so well. Would you like to return to the inn?" Larna was right — Maria was pale, even paler than she'd been yesterday.

But Maria shook her head. "No... I will be fine. However, everyone, I really do not want you entering that mansion..."

"What do you mean?"

"The presence I can see... the presence of darkness that's emanating from there... it's abnormal. I said as much yesterday, but this is a truly fearsome presence. It is more terrifying than anything I've seen before. And that feeling fills the entire mansion, as if the building itself is engulfed in darkness..." Maria looked at the building once again, only to start shivering once more. She soon wrapped her arms around herself to suppress her shivering.

Even I froze at Maria's words. But Sora was quick to follow up on her point. "I agree with Lady Maria, too. That mansion really does not feel right. While I may not be able to visually perceive it like the lady does... I feel shivers run down my spine. It is indeed a very dangerous place, I'm afraid."

Our party fell silent. A mansion filled with Dark Magic... I had never heard of anything so frightening. Maria's pale face and Sora's severe expression were more than enough to convince me to be wary of this place.

"...I suppose we have no choice, then. If it really is such a dangerous place, I don't have any plans or strategies to offer, for now. In any case, we should put some distance between us and the mansion, and then contact the Ministry."

Agreeing with Larna's decision, our small group quickly distanced ourselves from the horrible place.

Larna had mentioned contacting the Ministry, but for some reason, she led us to a tall building and went inside. We waited for her to return, waiting silently until finally Jeord spoke.

"Lady Maria... if it does not distress you, I would very much like to know. How was that presence at the mansion different from what you have seen up until now...?"

"Well... I find myself unable to explain it very well. But... if I had to put it into words... it was a very thick, heavy darkness."

"A thick darkness, you say?"

"Yes... The Dark Magic I saw before was almost a solid, black haze... a mist. And I have only seen it so concentrated in the small room where Raphael was during the school festival. That haze was dark and dense. It felt terrible. But this place..."

"Is worse, I gather?"

"Yes. The black haze I just saw simply dwarfs anything I've seen before. It is... incomparable. Terrifying," Maria said.

Sora quickly added his observations. "I, too, felt an incredible sense of danger from the place. Something that seemed to be telling me that I should not be anywhere near it."

"I see."

I quietly listened to their exchange. A presence of Dark Magic stronger than anything they had seen before. A place that would be far too dangerous to approach...

It wasn't too long before Larna stepped out of the building. "It is a very dangerous place, yes. I have called in reinforcements from the Ministry," she said. I had expected this, given how dangerous this whole thing had turned out to be. But then she added, "So we should all return to the inn and wait for them to come."

"Um, but Lady Larna," I blurted out quickly. "When will we go back to the mansion, then?"

Larna seemed troubled by my question. "Perhaps tomorrow or later. We have to wait for the reinforcements to get here, after all."

"...Tomorrow... or later." This place was filled with intense Dark Magic. Something terrible would happen if we tried to tackle it ourselves. But... if Keith was really being held there...

The image from my dream floated into my mind. The young boy had looked just like Keith. He was crying. While we waited, terrible things could be done to Keith. Maybe he was crying right now, just like when he was little.

"Um, Lady Larna..."

"What is it, Katarina?"

I stared straight into Larna's eyes as she turned to face me. "I... can't wait."

"But... that's..." Larna's eyes widened in surprise.

"I understand that it's a dangerous place. But... But if Keith is really there... there's no telling what could be done to him right now! We don't even know if Keith will be alive tomorrow morning!"

"..."

"Something terrible could happen to Keith before we get there... I can't just sit here and wait. I don't mind going alone if that's what it takes. Please, let me do this." I spoke strongly, in the only way I knew.

Larna seemed distressed, while Maria and Sora looked surprised. Maybe that was because they all knew that I had no real power of any kind. Even so, my dear brother was in trouble! He could be suffering at this very moment! There was no way I could simply wait.

I bit my lip, silently awaiting her response. That was when someone next to me spoke up.

"Lady Larna, please consider it."

"Huh…? Prince Jeord?" My eyes widened in surprise as I turned to him. After all, wasn't he absolutely against exposing me to any kind of danger? I would never in a million years have thought that he would approve of my proposal. With my mouth agape, I stared blankly at Jeord, who just gave me an uneasy smile in response.

Jeord then turned to Larna again. "It wouldn't only be Katarina. I would be with her as well. Please give us permission, Lady Larna."

"…Are you serious, Prince Jeord?"

Jeord responded to the still-shocked Larna with a serious expression and a nod. "Of course." Then he looked back at me. "You see, once Katarina has decided to resolve something, there's no stopping her. Even if you refused, she would surely attempt to break in on her own."

Jeord hit the nail on the head. I withdrew slightly at his accuracy. "Ugh…" He was right, though. That was exactly what I had in mind. I would have run off on my own even if Larna had refused.

Jeord flashed me a more reserved smile in response. "I understand your thoughts relatively well, Katarina."

"Hmm…" For a while, Larna was silent, alone in her thoughts. And then she finally said, "I suppose a quick rescue would be better, given how dangerous the situation is… but it wouldn't do for you two to just run off on your own." But judging by her expression, she

115

seemed to realize that she didn't have much of a choice in the matter. "Alright then. In light of your resolve, I suppose we should break in."

"Thank you, Lady Larna!" I literally jumped for joy.

"But we can't go right this second. After all, it's not like the place looks like it would welcome visitors. We have to survey the site first and identify possible points of entry." Larna turned to the young man who had been silently observing all this time. "Sora, could you pull it off?"

The edges of Sora's lips curled up at Larna's words. "Oh, but of course. Now that we have decided on a course of action, I will do everything in my power."

With that, Sora set off to scout the mansion and its premises. I thought that going alone would be dangerous, but he told me that he preferred working alone. "I am used to things like this, so leave it to me," he'd said as he flashed me a mischievous, almost boisterous grin and set off.

From everything I'd heard, Sora lived a life like the protagonist of a spy movie. I supposed it was best to let him do his thing. *He's a useful guy to have around…*

With Sora gone, the remainder of our party returned to a spot some distance away, waiting for his return.

"U-Um. Prince Jeord?"

"What is it, Katarina?"

I bowed my head. "Thank you for what you said just now. For… agreeing with what I said."

"Haha. I understand too well, Katarina, that once you have that expression about you, you are all but unstoppable," Jeord replied with a soft smile.

"…'That expression'?" *What is he talking about?*

"That face you make when it's time to resolve something."

"…Huh." I didn't understand what he meant. Perhaps my expressions were just easy to read?

Jeord merely smiled at my apparent confusion. "The truth of it is, Katarina… I already knew that you would say as much, when you blurted out that you would rush in and rescue Keith right away. You are, after all, simply that sort of person."

"Hm?"

"If there is someone in need, someone asking for help… you simply run straight to them, even if you are ill-equipped to handle such a task."

Does he mean that I'm impulsive? That I fly off the hook too easily? I withdrew slightly, feeling like I was being lectured.

"Ah, I'm not mad at you, Katarina," he said, still smiling faintly. "I quite like that part of you. For example… if I were the prisoner in question, instead of Keith, you would still rush in to save me in that very same manner, no?"

I still didn't understand what he was trying to say, but I had an immediate answer for his question. "Of course I would. No question." I nodded with conviction.

Judging from his grin, Jeord seemed pleased with my response. "Ah, Katarina. I really do like that about you," he said as he patted me on the head.

For some reason I found myself blushing, and my heart started beating a little faster.

"Haha… I hope you've steeled yourself, Katarina. Once this is all over…" He trailed off and didn't continue, instead just smiling vaguely.

"So they really came... As I expected."

"You say something, Sarah?" I asked. Sarah had been staring out of the window and muttering something I couldn't hear.

She just smiled in that charming way and answered, "Oh, it's nothing."

"That right?"

My name is Thomas Coleman. It had been a month since I had met this woman called Sarah. At first I thought she was shady, but now I felt like she was the only one who understood me. I trusted her completely.

I was supposed to be the heir to the Coleman family. I would have been the viscount. I should have been raised like the special guy I was, like the heir I was born to be. But that was stolen from me by my younger brother. They even chased me out of the house.

It was a completely unbelievable thing to happen. In the first place, I didn't do anything wrong. The reason I didn't do well in school was because my tutors were useless. And all my servants kept quitting, 'cause they were useless, too. The people around me were no good. I didn't do anything wrong.

My own father looked at me in shock and said, *"How did it come to this?"* He looked down on me. Me! It was humiliating to be stared at like that by that man. That womanizer.

And then there was my younger brother, who started following that man around. He looked down on me the same way, even though he should have been following me around. *"Why don't you think about the things you've done?"* he'd say.

I was unlucky. It was all bad luck. For me to have a father like that, and a brother like that. It's because I was surrounded by these goons that I couldn't reach my true potential.

Since I was down on my luck, I just wallowed in it. Never did anything other than smack around some of those idiot servants. Before I knew it, I'd lost everything, and got chased out of the house.

I was given a bit of coin when I got kicked out, but that was soon used up. All I could do was bemoan my pathetic existence in the equally lousy home I was given. It was then I thought that I'd wander into town and get my hands on some booze... when I saw him.

I had never seen him since leaving my family's home all those years ago. From what the rumors said though, he was taken in by some duke and was living large with society's elite. When I heard that, I was pissed off. What was he doing, strutting around like that? He was nothing more than the child of a whore. But I was never part of the world of nobles, so I never saw him with my own eyes. Eventually, I forgot about that too.

Now that I had lost everything, I never thought I'd see the day where I actually saw him in person. My younger brother, Keith Claes. We didn't even have the same mother. Of course not. His mother was a filthy whore. Disgusting.

But he didn't care about his status. He attacked me with his magic, even. He dropped a bunch of hard rocks on my head. I was severely injured and even broke some bones. It was so terrifying that I even had nightmares about him.

He was terrifying, but at the same time I hated him. Keith really was the worst. Useless trash. How could a guy like him wear such nice clothes? Why was a woman next to him? What's up with that happy smile of his? All that while I was made to wear dirty clothing, forced to live hand-to-mouth... while he gets to take advantage of a duke's fortunes, living exorbitantly with women waiting on him? Unforgivable. All that just because he had some magical power. Just that, and he got taken in by a duke.

Keith is nothing... nothing more than some whoreson. Why, then?! Why only him...?

Unforgivable. Can't forgive him. Unforgivable.

I want to bring him down to where I am. No... worse. Worse than that. A guy like that... he should just be a slave in some foreign place.

The more I looked at how Keith was now, the more I thought that way. Those thoughts took over my mind. But I didn't have any status or coin. I was pissed off, but I couldn't do shit.

And the days passed... and passed. Until one day, that woman appeared before me.

"Wah, that jet-black, abysmally dark heart of yours... Could you tell me a bit about yourself, hmm?"

"Hm?"

A voice, from that black-haired woman, called out to me when I was wandering through town. At first, I didn't know what she was talking about. I was surprised. But then I remembered... she was someone I knew, who often brought my alcohol. So I told her everything.

About how I couldn't reach my true potential because of my useless tutors. About my stupid womanizing father. About how I was chased away from my own home because of my stupid, foolish brother. And how I saw my other brother, born to a different mother, after all these years...

"Why? Why does a monster like that, with that dirty blood, get to enjoy all that's good in life? Why does he get a good social standing? Why am I the only unfortunate one, the unlucky one, while he gets it all? I'll never forgive him."

The woman named Sarah, unlike the others, didn't look upon me with pity when I uttered my curses. "It really is as you say. What an unfortunate man you are," she said.

Until now, no one had actually listened to what I had to say. Guess they were all stupid. All talentless hacks and goons. She was different. For the first time in my life, I finally met someone who understood me.

I continued to tell Sarah all about myself after that. And then I said, "I want Keith to fall to the pits, just like me. I want to see him become nothing more than a pathetic, helpless slave... writhing on the ground."

"That's right... If you do that, the pain in your heart will heal, perhaps..." She smiled faintly. Sarah was around my age, from what I could tell. But her smile was like that of a child's. It was... adorable. Before I knew it, I had handed Sarah everything. My heart included.

Sarah didn't say very much. I didn't know who she really was, but it seemed like she had a lot of money and a good position in society. I moved from that lousy home, which was given to me as some sort of compensation when I was kicked out of the family, to some huge mansion in a town I'd never heard of. The place was furnished, and Sarah even prepared proper clothes for me.

"These fixtures and clothing are much more suitable for the true you, don't you think?" she said. Even the servants, too. They weren't useless, like my family's. These guys were very capable. They all listened to me. I regained everything I'd lost... all thanks to meeting Sarah.

And that wasn't all. Sarah would go on and grant every single one of my wishes.

"Hey, I've gone and fetched Keith Claes. You may do with him as you please."

Sarah led me to a room... and there he was. His limbs restrained to a bed frame. He looked dirty, his hair in disarray. He looked nothing like the person I saw in town back then.

That's good. That's what you get, you whoreson. Put on airs, will you? Becoming the heir of a duke doesn't suit you... but this does.

After some time had passed, Sarah told me he had come to. I headed over to the room once more. When I entered, Keith had already woken up.

I stood in front of him. "Been a while."

At my voice, his blue eyes turned to me. I remember feeling irritated. He was in this situation, and he still looked at me like that? For a while after that, he didn't react. He just kept looking at me with those eyes.

Back when we used to live under the same roof, he would never dare keep quiet when I spoke to him. And here he was. Silently looking at me. That made me even more angry.

This guy... it's because he became a duke's heir! He must think he's some big shot now!

"Yeah, don't say anything, then. Guess you don't want to say anything to lower-class nobles, huh!" I shouted at him, almost spitting out the words.

His eyes seemed to widen. "...Thomas?" And he said my name.

Even if he was my half-brother... he was a whoreson. He was sent to live with us because it'd be less troublesome that way. That's why he always had to address us in the correct way, with the appropriate titles. We were his superiors.

He was supposed to do that... and now look at him. It's only been a few years since I've seen him, and he's forgotten all about it.

It's like he's looking down on me. Like I'm inferior to him. I could feel something inside me snapping.

I swung my fist down on the man restrained on the rickety bed. "D-Don't you dare... someone like you... say my name so freely! SOMEONE LIKE YOU!"

You dare?! The likes of you, look down on me?

You're supposed to be beneath me... just something beneath me. But now... you've come out on top.

Why did I fall so far? Why am I the only unfortunate one?

I kept swinging my fists. I kept hitting him. His limbs were restrained... and Sarah did something to him to seal up his magic. He couldn't fight back.

But then... no matter how much I hit him, Keith never once cried out in pain. He didn't ask for mercy or forgiveness. All he did was remain silent. His eyes were unwavering... as silent and still as he was.

It was like I wasn't even reflected in those eyes. Like he didn't even care. That pissed me off more. I hit him with my fists again and again and again. I couldn't stop.

Eventually, my fists started hurting, so I stopped. But Keith's expression didn't change. I hated him. But no matter how much I hit him, I didn't feel any better. In fact, I only felt more pathetic. Even as I thought about how he was about to be sold into slavery in some foreign place, it didn't make me feel any better. Not one bit.

Come to think of it... lately I'd felt my body becoming heavier. For some reason, waking up was hard. I noticed that I was sleeping a lot more. Sarah was considerate. She even gave me a shoulder massage, but it didn't help much. If anything, I seemed to be getting worse.

It was a strange feeling. As if someone else was taking something from me. Something important. Even so... when I felt up to it, I would go over to where Keith was locked up. I wanted to make him feel the pain, listen to his pleas and howls... but he never did any of that. He was silent, just like how he had been in the beginning.

No matter how much I struck him, no matter how much I yelled at him, his blue eyes never lost their shine. I only felt more pathetic as time passed.

"I'm not going to bother waiting for him to fall into the pits and be a slave anymore. I don't need him. Someone like that... he can just go and break for all I care," I said.

In response, Sarah asked, "Well then, should I do with him as I please?" She was smiling like usual.

"Yeah. Do as you like," I replied.

Sarah left the room happily.

Meanwhile, I felt my body becoming even heavier. As if I was slowly... losing something...

Sora finally returned from his scouting, and the time had finally come for us to break into that mansion. Since Maria was so frightened, she was told not to overexert herself and to return to the inn, but...

"No... I cannot possibly allow only Lady Katarina and everyone else into that mansion. I am a Wielder of Light... I'm sure I could be useful for something." Maria then took my hand. "And... with Lady Katarina by my side, I will be alright no matter what happens. With her here... I find myself able to face any enemy, no matter how ferocious or terrifying." Maria ended her statement with a slight smile.

I tightened my grip around Maria's hand. "Thank you, Maria. I'll be counting on you, too."

And so Larna, Jeord, Maria, Sora and I — five of us in total — headed back toward the mansion.

We decided to enter from the back entrance, since the security there was lighter. Even so, there were still three of those muscular goons standing on guard.

"So what do we do from here?" I asked, turning to Sora as we surveyed the mansion from a comfortable distance.

"Perhaps we should wait and see." This was Sora's mysterious response, which was accompanied by a grin.

But he was right. We waited for a while in silence and then, out of nowhere, there was a commotion among the guards. Two of the three men ran off immediately, though I had no idea where they were going.

"What happened?" I asked.

Sora responded calmly and innocently. "If I had to guess, a particular shed in the corner of the manor's gardens most likely caught fire."

"Eh… that's…"

"That would be my doing, of course. We should proceed now that security has been thinned."

Looking at Sora and his nonchalant expression, I felt immensely impressed with him once again.

The remaining guard suffered a more unfortunate fate — Larna hurled some sort of projectile at him with her powers of Wind Magic. It promptly hit him in the head, knocking him out cold in an instant.

"That went well," Larna said casually. This woman, too, was terribly impressive.

With that, our small group successfully infiltrated the mansion.

We were inside, and as I expected, the interior was just as gorgeous as the exterior. But I had to say, in my opinion, it was kind of overkill. Even the various art pieces on display seemed pointlessly flamboyant, so much so that it seemed like the person who'd chosen them had no taste. It seemed like the place belonged to a "new money" kind of person who just really liked shiny things.

Larna had mentioned that the governor of this area probably lived here. *Hmm, I wonder what kind of person they are?* An image of an individual covered in glittering gold necklaces came to mind. This person would be wearing something like a bathrobe and would be swirling a cup of red wine in his hand. That's what I was thinking about as we cautiously progressed down the new-money mansion's halls.

As expected of a grandiose mansion such as this one, there were many guards on the inside, too. We ran into them a few times, and sometimes where there was no place to hide, Sora would just raise his fist, and a moment later, the guard would be on the ground — out cold without a sound.

Other times, Larna would cast some unknown spell with a wave of her hand, and the guard would be sent flying. He would soon be out cold on the ground — without a sound, of course.

And then there was Jeord, who used a quick pommel strike with his blade. This would cause the guard on the receiving end to collapse onto the ground — again, without a sound.

There were times when the three of them couldn't control the force of their attacks. In those cases, Maria stepped in to heal minor scrapes and bruises with her Light Magic.

Looking at all this from a distance, I felt moved by the sheer power of my party members. If this was like one of those RPGs I played in my previous life, this was surely the most powerful party possible in the game. Split into classes, Larna would be the mage, Jeord the swordsman, Sora the soldier or rogue, and Maria the priestess. In that case, Keith, who was being held captive, would be the princess.

With all those class roles sorted out, I started picturing all of them as characters on the cover art of an RPG. That kept my mind busy as we went deeper and deeper into the mansion, with the gaudiness of the decor increasing the further we went. Although we had faced nothing but small fries until now, this would be a good place for a mid-boss to appear.

Just when that thought crossed my mind...

A nearby door opened with a slight creak, and out came a man. Our eyes met. "Wh-Who are you people?!"

I felt like I'd heard that phrase from somewhere specific before. But here he was: that pompous, new-money-rich old man I'd been imagining ever since setting foot in here. I mean, not exactly. He was dressed in fancy clothing, but he didn't have a puffy bathrobe or a glass of red wine. Well, considering it was only around noon, walking around in a bathrobe and drinking wine might have been odd.

In any case, the scene played out just as I imagined it would. There were a few burly men behind him — his personal bodyguards, probably. The gaudily-dressed old man immediately turned to them. "I-Intruders! Get them!" he shouted.

I could hear the random encounter music of that one RPG I liked playing in my mind. As expected of the flunkies of the mid-boss (that new-money old man), they were somewhat stronger than the mooks our party had been facing up until now. But still, they were no match for us. In a series of quick movements, Larna, Sora, and Jeord had silenced them. Soon, they lay in a heap on the ground.

It really was over in an instant. This party was simply too strong. It was like a bunch of level 99 characters walked into a level 1 dungeon.

With the new-money old man left alone, Sora swiftly cornered him and drew a knife seemingly from thin air. "So you own this place, huh?" he asked in a low voice.

All the old man could do was nod vigorously, his face pale. Yep, it was just as I imagined. This old man was the so-called governor of this area. *So this is the mid-boss or maybe the final boss? Hmm. Seriously, how underwhelming. The way he's squirming about, he seems more like a small-time crook. What a lame final boss.*

"Then ya know where Keith Claes is, right?" Sora said while ensuring the knife in his hand was visible.

The more I thought about it, the less this old man seemed to be the final boss. If he was really who he claimed to be, then we had this in the bag — all we had to do was find out where Keith was being held, and that was that.

"K-Keith Claes, you say? Who is that? I don't know anything about that name!" the old man said, desperately shaking his head.

"Won't do you much good keepin' it to yourself..." Sora said, approaching the old man somewhat menacingly, knife drawn.

What little color remaining in his face instantly disappeared. "N-No idea! I have no idea!" he said, continuing to shake his head this way and that.

Larna soon stepped up. "This won't take long. You lot wait here." With that, she entered the room the old man had come out from, with Sora following and dragging the unwilling old man.

After a while, they came back out of the room. "Unfortunately this old man really has no idea," Larna sighed.

I stole a peek into the room and saw that the gaudily-dressed old man was out cold on the ground. *I wonder what happened in there?*

While I was somewhat curious, I decided that it would probably be best not to think too hard about it.

As I pulled my thoughts away from that subject, Larna continued. "Also, this guy was under the influence of Dark Magic. He was being controlled by someone."

"Huh?! But isn't he the most important person in this mansion? He was the mastermind, right?" I had been thinking that the old, unimpressive-looking man was the final boss, but it turned out that I was wrong!

"Well, it does seem that he owns the mansion, that much is true. However, he doesn't seem to be involved in what happened to Keith. They probably used the Dark Arts on him so they could use his home for the kidnapping." Then she turned to Maria and asked, "Could you confirm this, Maria?"

Maria checked the room and then came back and said, "It is true, I can see remnants of Dark Magic around the old man. It's separate from the aura surrounding the house."

So, that new-money old man was just being controlled, and wasn't the real mastermind, huh? So that means the villain behind this and Keith are both still somewhere out there.

"But Alexander is still pointing toward something. Do you sense anything, Maria?"

"Yes. The churning, dark mist grows thicker the more we progress through these halls… there may very well be something at the end of all this."

After hearing Larna's and Maria's observations, our party decided to go deeper into the mansion. Once we passed the new-money old man's room, the art pieces on display were no longer obnoxiously flamboyant. The atmosphere actually felt somewhat… lonely. The halls were empty and dark.

"Ugh… the mist is really getting… thicker…" Maria said, placing a hand over her mouth in a seemingly involuntary action.

"Yeah… this place is bad news," Sora agreed. Then he muttered under his breath, "Just how much mana capacity does this guy have…?"

"Mana capacity? What's that?"

"Precisely what it seems, Lady Katarina. Our mana is not infinite. If we use up too much, it will dry up, will it not?"

"Well, yeah, but it comes back after some rest, right?"

As Sora said, mana could be used up. Every person had a different amount in them, but that didn't change the fact that using it would cause that amount to go down. But then it would naturally recover when the person took a rest, just the same as physical stamina.

"That is correct. But you see, that only holds true for the five elements. Dark Magic is different; as you use it, the amount of mana goes down and it never recovers."

"Oh!" This was shocking to me. I continued listening to Sora with my eyes wide.

"Even Raphael, who used to wield Dark Magic, confirmed this after some testing. Dark Magic is very much a finite resource. So you see, to be able to use it on so many people like this is quite a feat."

"Then… is the Wielder of Darkness here someone really strong?"

Then they're totally the final boss, right?! Even the strongest party wouldn't have any hopes of victory…

"…I have no idea. It is a terrifying level of mana for one person to have, certainly. But there may be a few of them, if you think about it…"

A few Wielders of Darkness all in the same place… that was quite a terrifying prospect.

"Either way, we're grasping at straws if we don't keep at it."

"R-Right..." I suppose it was a given that it was terrifying to wonder about the unknown. *Yes, we should keep going.*

And the party did just that. Eventually, we came to a large door that was made of metal or some other sturdy material. If this were an RPG, this would be the door to the final boss's chambers.

Ugly Bear pointed confidently at the door, as if to say that Keith was being held within. But I couldn't rely on just that stupid thing for a true answer, so I turned to Maria.

"Beyond this door is... a most terrifying presence of Dark Magic..." she said.

"Yes, this place feels very dangerous. It is certainly the source," added Sora. They both had severe expressions on their faces.

In that case, the final boss was probably here. And Keith would be there too.

The party and I — well, just the party actually — took some time making preparations, and then we all went through the sturdy door. And behind that door, in the room filled with the swirling mists of Dark Magic...

...Was nothing. There was no final boss waiting for us there. In fact, this seemed like just some kind of guest parlor. In the middle of the room was a table, and around it, some chairs. A very simple setup.

I had been steeling myself for an impressive and terrifying room all this time... so I was let down horribly. Hanging back at the entrance, I peered around, but there was no one there! I couldn't feel the presence of any living being. *Eh...? Maybe this isn't the final boss's chambers, after all...?*

With that in mind, I stepped in, only to see something in the corner of the room. The furnishings had been blocking our view — but now I saw that a man was collapsed in the corner.

"Eeek! Wh-What?!" I involuntarily let out a squeal at the sight of him, but there was no reaction from the man in the corner.

Sora approached the man cautiously, calling out to him as he did so. "Oi… you!" But there was no response. He shook the man in an attempt to wake him.

Wow. That's really something… The man did wake up, and I was surprised by what I saw. He seemed very plump when he was collapsed in a heap, but now that I looked at him better, I saw that it was much more than that.

He had messy hair and an incredibly fleshy body. Even the features of his face were buried in fat, and his skin was glistening and oily. He was quite the sight. For some reason, this person really looked like he'd play the role of a villain in any production or game.

Since he was on the ground, I had assumed that he was a victim of some kind, but a look at his face was enough for me to realize that he was up to no good. *Well… I suppose I have a villainess face too, so I'm hardly one to judge, but…*

"Oi. You. Are you okay?" Sora said after checking that the man's eyes were open.

"Guh…" was all he had to say. It would seem like the large man was alive, at least. What a relief.

"I don't see any wounds on ya, but you're definitely weak. Who are you?"

The man's eyes seemed to open somewhat wider at Sora's question, although it was difficult to tell due to his engorged features. But he didn't say or do anything else. All he did was stare into space endlessly.

Hmm. It doesn't seem like we'll be able to hold much of a conversation with him. That's what I thought, anyway.

"Hey, do you live here? Do you know where Keith Claes is?" I asked, although I wasn't expecting much of an answer.

"...Keith," the man said. His previously unfocused eyes trained onto a single thing in the room — a shelf in the corner. "...That whoreson... monster. I have to see him kick the bucket..." With those violent words, the man propped himself up, pushing Sora's arms away. His eyes stayed focused on what was immediately in front of him.

All we could do at this sudden development was stare as the man slowly moved across the room, eventually making his way to the shelf, and then placing his hand on its side. With that, the shelf slid away to the side, revealing a hidden door.

What's this? A secret passage? I felt like I had seen something like this during the school festival incident, too. More importantly... I was now sure that Keith was just beyond this door.

"Kick it... See him kick the bucket..." The man continued to mutter his slurred threats. Before I knew it, Jeord had approached him.

What's going on?

Jeord turned to the man and raised his sword.

"GAH!" the man spat, and a moment later he was down on the ground.

"Surely he has identified himself as a hostile, from his very own words. I suppose we have heard enough, no?" Jeord said, sheathing his sword with the darkest of smiles on his face.

"...Well. Yes, I suppose that's fine." Larna nodded.

Huh?! That's fine? Well... I guess he really was saying some terrible things

"But from what he was saying, we can be sure that Keith is beyond this point. He may be in danger," Larna continued, looking grim. Then she announced, "We have to hurry. We're breaching and entering."

She pushed on the door and Jeord and Sora both drew their weapons, preparing for a potential ambush.

With a loud creak, the door swung open. The room didn't seem to have any windows — it was completely dark, so the only light was from the room we were in. There were no windows, no table, chairs, not even a bed. It was like some sort of dungeon.

And then, collapsed in the corner of the room was... someone. The light flooding in from the door illuminated this person. His hair was muddy, and his clothes were filthy. Although he looked nothing like how he usually did, I instantly recognized him. He was the person I had been searching for all this time... someone dear to me.

"Keith!" I shouted, immediately rushing to his side.

Someone from behind me told me to be careful or something like that, but I didn't hear much of it. "Keith, Keith! Are you alright?! Wake up!" I knelt down, holding Keith in my arms — and that was when I noticed the countless bruises on his face.

I felt my heart breaking from what I saw. Keith's face was pale and he was cold to the touch. *I-It can't be!* I felt my blood freeze in my veins.

I quickly put my ear by his lips. Although it was faint, I clearly heard Keith's breathing. *What a relief Keith is alive!* I sighed as a deep sense of relief washed over me. "He's alive! Keith is alive!"

"I see. That's wonderful, Katarina," Jeord said, standing next to me. He seemed genuinely relieved too. "But you feel no ill effects, touching that mist?" he asked, sounding surprised.

Mist? What mist? I followed Jeord's gaze, and, "Wha?! Wh-What's this?"

My surprise almost caused me to drop Keith in shock. An unbelievable sight was before my eyes — there was mud all over Keith, yes, but there was something else, too. A black, mist-like substance was wrapped all around him. It was like a long snake of some kind had entwined itself around his limbs and abdomen.

"P-Prince Jeord... what is this?"

"I haven't the slightest idea. However... it would seem that you are unharmed, even if you do come into contact with it. I had thought to warn you, to tell you that it might be dangerous and not to rush in... but of course, you were never one to listen."

"...Ah." I hadn't noticed it at all. I guess I heard him say something, maybe? Anyway, my spirits were high now that I had finally found Keith. I supposed I just hadn't heard Jeord's warnings or seen the black mist around him.

As I calmed down a bit, I looked around the room and saw Maria holding onto the door for support, her knees trembling and her face pale. Sora wasn't faring any better — he had the same kind of expression on his face, and was backed up against the wall as far as he could go. Even Larna was standing far away, her hand raised cautiously. She was absolutely silent, like she was ready to cast a spell at a moment's notice.

Even Jeord, who had approached me, seemed skittish. Was he simply being cautious... or was this black, misty object too visually similar to the one thing he was afraid of in the world?

"Apparently you're unharmed by it, Katarina. Maria, Sora, are you two alright?" Larna said, after confirming that I was unhurt. She turned to her subordinates for an answer, only for the two of them to shake their heads.

"I-I'm alright... but I cannot... approach. Any further. My sincere apologies..." Maria stuttered, her face the palest shade I had ever seen it.

"I am the same. I feel a powerful magical force; I cannot get any closer. Not more than this." Sora's fear, made obvious by the sweat on his brow, was the real thing.

So from what I had gathered, this mist was the source of that strange hazy aura filling the mansion. It was giving off a strong magical effect, to the point where Maria and Sora couldn't even approach it. In fact, it was so strong that someone like me, who normally couldn't detect Dark Magic, could see it with my own eyes.

"Then… does this mean that Keith has had Dark Magic cast on him?" I thought that must be why these black tendrils were all over him.

"I… I believe that is the case, Lady Katarina," Maria replied, occasionally stuttering.

I see. In that case…

"Keith! Wake up! It's me, Katarina! I've come to get you!" I was almost shouting as I called out to Keith.

I had been told that Dark Magic could only be dispelled by the caster, but I knew better. After all, I had dispelled it before on my own. So there was only one thing to do: I had to inspire Keith to defeat this magic from within, by his own power.

Back then, when I had been put to sleep with Dark Magic, everyone called out to me, and that was how I managed to break free. That was how I won. Surely it must be the same way for Keith — if I called out to him, he would surely wake up, too.

It was with those thoughts in mind that I desperately called out to him. I shook him slightly, still cradling him in my arms. "We've found you, we've come to get you! Wake up, Keith…" And then, "I won't cause any more trouble for you Keith, I promise, so wake up…" I kept calling out to him, again and again.

Everyone else pitched in, too. Even so…

"Why won't you wake up, Keith…?" No matter how much we called out to him, he didn't move an inch. For some reason, his breath became even shallower, and his hand even colder to the touch.

"I have to see him kick the bucket..." I remembered what that hollow-eyed man had said. *Is Keith going to die if this goes on...?*

"...Why? Why isn't it working...? Why?"

As she continued watching my futile attempts, Maria lamented, "Perhaps the Dark Magic cast on him was too strong... and Master Keith is unable to break out of it by his own power..."

"In that case... can't we get the caster to dispel it? Who is this person, anyway...?!"

It seemed like the hollow-eyed man we had seen earlier was not the original caster of this dark mist. In that case, who was this Wielder of Darkness? We didn't know. Was there really nothing we could do? *If this goes on, Keith will...!*

A strong, resolute voice soon cut through the atmosphere of despair. "Then we have to find them."

I looked up and saw determination in Larna's eyes.

"To use such a huge amount of magic, and to control everyone else... this mystery person must have some sort of plan. This was why they still haven't shown themselves. The enemy is probably still in this mansion, or at least close by. Maria, Sora, and I shall conduct this search. In the meantime... Katarina and Prince Jeord, stay with Keith until we return."

With that, Larna patted me on the head a few times in a reassuring fashion. I could feel my despair slightly ebbing. "Yes... Please do everything you can," I said, bowing my head deeply in Larna's direction.

"Well then, Prince Jeord. I leave the two of them in your care."

Larna left with Maria and Sora following close behind her. The trio once again commenced their search for this mystery Wielder of Darkness.

After the three of them had left, I turned my attention back to Keith and kept calling out to him. *Maybe he'll wake up now,* I thought. But there was still no reaction from my brother.

Although I had been discouraged, although I sank into the depths of despair at first… I was now upset. I was angry. *Why did this happen to my dear brother? Who would do this to him?*

Perhaps it was a bit biased for an adoptive older sister like me to say, but Keith really was a wonderful person. He was kind and gentle to everyone. Why, then, did he have to go through all this? To suffer this much? This was unfair. Too unfair.

I could feel the anger rising up from within me.

To hell with Dark Magic! Why would something like that be cast on my cute brother! I'll never forgive this Wielder of Darkness or whatever the hell they are! Once I find them, I'm going to take this lousy black mist and wrap them up in it, just like they did to Keith!

Actually, this black snake thing wrapping itself around Keith is probably the reason why he's still not waking up, isn't it?!

This stupid black thing is too long! Some snake it is, it doesn't even look the part! Urrgghhh! I'm so mad!

Something like this… I should just pull it off and toss it into some river!

Just when my rage had hit its peak, I felt a strange source of heat from the right side of my waist. Right where my pocket was.

It was so hot that for a second I thought a burning piece of coal had been placed in my pocket. I stuck my hand into it and pulled out the strange mirror-looking disc that Jeord had gifted me with a few days ago.

Ah, Jeord bought this for me, didn't he? I had forgotten all about it. But as soon as I touched the disc, the black mist began to solidify. I could see it a lot clearer now, though I didn't know why.

Huh? Why? Actually, I can see it very, very well.

In fact, I feel like I could hold it in my hands. I wanted to grab it off Keith and toss it somewhere — maybe I could actually do exactly that now.

I reached out toward a loop of the black mist. Although it had been translucent and immaterial earlier, I could now clearly feel it in my hand.

I can do this! I gripped the black mist tightly. Then I started to mercilessly tear loops of it off of Keith, tossing them onto the ground next to him with a flourish. "Ha! Take that!"

Jeord, who had been standing next to me all this time, watched on with his mouth agape. The mist that had been ripped off now wriggled helplessly on the muddy ground, looking like a bunch of black snakes. As a final gesture, I gathered all of the mist together with my free hand before relentlessly crushing each and every single one in my fist.

The mist seemed to condense into a droplet around the size of a person's fist — and then, it stopped moving.

Oh-ho. I guess that black mist does become a variety of shapes after all. If only it had become some sort of cute shape, like a puppy or something, I might have even showed it some degree of mercy.

Well, that aside…

"I suppose that's that! Done and done."

Shifting his eyes to the now immobile, fist-shaped droplet, the frozen Jeord seemingly snapped out of his trance. "What?! Wh-What was that, Katarina?! What have you done?" He had completely lost his usual confident smile and refined manner of speaking.

Just as his horrified and surprised expression nearly got the best of me… I heard a familiar voice from the person I had been cradling in my arms. "U-Ugh…"

139

"Ah!" A reaction from Keith!

Soon enough… Keith opened his eyes. At first, his blue eyes seemed to be wandering, lost amongst the stars… before they finally focused upon me.

"Big… Sister…" he said in a soft, trembling voice.

This was unmistakably Keith's voice — one I had not heard for days.

"…Keith!" I hugged my brother, who I was still cradling in my arms, tight.

It was a cold, dark place. I kept absolutely quiet, and absolutely still. For that was how I should be.

My first memory was doing exactly as I was told by my mother, hugging my knees in a dark room. *Shut up and just stay there!*

I would be given food at irregular intervals. I ate what I was given, bit by bit. If I ate it all at once, I would have nothing left. By rationing it out, I could bear with the hunger for just a little bit longer.

When I began to gain a sense of self and learn a little more about the world, I learned that I was an unnecessary existence in the eyes of my mother.

Soon enough, I was three years old. Someone claiming to be my father told me I would move in with my brothers — born to a different mother, apparently. But I was unwanted and unneeded there, too.

At first, they would call me names like "son of a prostitute" and "whoreson." And when I injured my brothers with my magic, they called me "monster." I spent my days alone in my room, doing as little as I possibly could. I pretended that I didn't exist.

Yes, that was how I had lived. I lived alone, in that room, never making myself known to anyone. I was unwanted. I was not needed by anyone. And that was why I wouldn't mind even if I were to disappear in this cold, dark place.

I was afraid of the darkness at first. I shivered and cried. Tears flowed down my cheeks. But now... it almost felt comforting. Soothing. I felt like I wouldn't mind at all if I were to just dissolve into the darkness without a sound.

I was unwanted, unneeded, right? What did I live for? To be abused? To put up with extreme acts of violence...? That would hardly be worth living for. Just as that thought crossed my mind...

"...Keith."

I felt like someone said my name.

It was my name, I guess. The name that was given to me. But few called me by it...

Who could it be, I wonder? It was such a familiar voice.

I looked around me... and yet, there was nothing but an endless expanse of darkness. Perhaps I was just imagining things.

Yes... it must have been nothing more than my imagination. There was no one in this world who would so gently say my name.

I curled up once more. I stilled my breathing. I would disappear, melt into the darkness, just like this.

"...Keith."

That voice, once more. I could hear it much more clearly now.

"...Who is it...?" I replied to the unseen voice in the darkness.

I looked around again. As I expected, there was no one there. However, I soon heard that voice again.

"Keith, wake up!"

It was a voice I had heard before... somewhere. It was a very, very familiar voice. And yet... I did not know who it belonged to.

"…Who? Who are you?" I asked again.

"Keith, it's me! I've come to get you!"

Come to… get me? Nonsense. No one would do that for me. After all, all of them abused me. My mother, father, even those brothers of mine, born to a different mother. *Who is this person…? It's no good. I cannot remember a thing.*

I held my head in a mixture of confusion and frustration. Indeed, I was abused. I was mistreated. I was cast aside like trash. And yet… I felt like I was forgetting something very important every time I heard this voice. Just as I thought I would remember… the darkness snatched that thought from me.

"Keith… hey. Open your eyes…"

That voice desperately called out to me, again and again.

Ah… do I have someone like that, too? Someone who would say my name in such a fashion…?

I want to remember. I want to know… But the darkness hindered my thoughts. It tempted me. That it was fine to never remember, that it was fine to just sink into the darkness as I was. It would be much easier to just surrender, as opposed to thinking about it all… or so I thought.

"Keith!"

That voice. It simply wouldn't stop. As if it was telling me not to go there. Not to go into the darkness. Should I surrender myself to the darkness… or should I listen to the voice? I did not know. I was at a loss.

It was then that a single speck of light appeared in this world of darkness. *What… is that?* I kept staring at the light. As I did so, it slowly expanded. Slowly but surely… the memories returned to my mind.

"Hello, you are Keith, yes? Welcome to the Claes family."

The spring when I turned eight, that was what I was told as I was brought before a woman and a girl with aqua-blue eyes.

"Call me Big Sister!" the girl had said, beaming at me. And then she took me outside the house, and taught me many, many things.

Even so… I ended up accidentally hurting her with my magic. I was unable to control it. I was sure she hated me after that. I would be mistreated and abused once again, I was so sure.

The girl, however… forgave me. With a smile on her face. And then she said to me the words I wanted to hear the most.

"Let's stay together from now on!"

Ahh… how could I have forgotten?

With that, I remembered. All of it, everything, all at once. My adoptive parents — my capable and noble father, and my gentle and loving mother. The kind and caring servants, too… my dear friends, who accepted me with all of their being. And the person I loved most in the world… my adoptive sister, Katarina Claes.

It was true. Up until that spring when I turned eight, I did not mean a thing to anyone. But I was different now. Now, I had many people who cared about me. Important people. Should I disappear… they would surely mourn me.

I had also made up my mind that I would stay next to Katarina, and I would do everything I could to protect her. And so, I couldn't just disappear. I could not simply be swallowed by the darkness.

I raised my head — and before I knew it, I was enveloped by a warm, soothing light. The darkness that I had been lost in before… was now all but gone.

As I slowly opened my eyes, awakened by that gentle sensation... her face came into view. The face of the person I loved the most. Her aqua-blue eyes stared straight into mine. Large tears were falling from her eyes.

I found myself cradled in Katarina's arms. She was the first one to hold me in such a way... ever since I had become aware of myself. It happened when I tried my best to catch Katarina as she fell from a tree, and then lost consciousness from the impact. She held me so tightly. And just like now, tears flowed from her eyes as she continued to worry about me. It was then that I first understood the kindness and gentleness of others. My chest felt warm, then.

Ah... I'm dreaming about my childhood. Although Katarina did do that a lot as a child, our mother was somewhat strict with her as we got a little older. As time passed, she eventually stopped hugging me so casually.

However... Katarina was much older in this dream. In fact, she looked just like I remembered. Even the soft sensation of her skin felt different. It was nothing like when we were children. Was this just a dream of my desires, then? After all... I was incredibly envious of how Prince Jeord touched Katarina however and whenever he pleased, on account of him being her fiancé.

"...Big Sister..." I said.

"Keith!" Katarina sounded happy. She held me tightly. "I'm so glad you're okay... so glad...!" she mumbled, burying her tear-streaked face into my chest.

Katarina never really did grow very tall. To think that we would be embracing like this, at such a distance... *Ah... what a blissful dream.* I hadn't had any such pleasant dreams as of late.

"Keith, are you alright?" Perhaps Katarina found my blissful silence strange. She looked at me with a surprised expression. Her glistening, aqua-blue eyes… so lovely. How else would I describe them?

If this were reality, I would not be able to handle the embarrassment. I would surely have pushed her away. This was just a dream, though… and so I guessed a little more contact wouldn't hurt. To make up for what I could not do in reality…

"Keith?"

I placed a single hand on Katarina's face, before placing my lips against her tear-stained cheek. As she stared at me, frozen in place… I slowly moved my lips toward hers.

Soon enough, my lips were against hers — her lovely, pink, adorable lips. They were softer than I'd imagined.

For a while, I thoroughly enjoyed the softness of her lips, before finally pulling away. Her face was flushed red, and she was frozen in one of her amusing expressions.

Ahh… Katarina really is adorable, just as I've always thought. In fact, she was probably more adorable than anything I had imagined, or was capable of imagining.

"Ah… what a nice dream, truly…" I muttered as I felt my eyelids become impossibly heavy.

It was a little strange for me to feel sleepy, considering that I was already in a dream… but there was little I could do to ward off the sensation. Soon enough, I felt myself sinking into a deep, deep sleep…

Huh? What was that? What just happened?

I was frozen in place, unable to comprehend what had just happened, as usual.

Hmm. Let's go through the chain of events leading up to this point. First, I thought of tilling the fields back at Claes Manor to increase my magical powers... no, that was a little too far back. Let's try this again. After all, it would take a long time to summarize events from my childhood up to this point in time.

Ugh, that wasn't it! Remember, Katarina! Think of what just happened a while ago! Firstly... we got to this room, and found the missing Keith. But Dark Magic had been cast on him, and he wouldn't wake up no matter how much I called to him. That was why Larna and the rest left in search of the individual who cast the spell. Only Jeord and I were left in this room.

But no matter how much or how loudly I called to Keith, he didn't react at all! And so I got really angry and said, "Why? Why does Keith have to suffer like this?!"

And then I felt that mirror that Jeord bought for me heating up. And then I touched it, and felt that I could do something about that black mist-snake. *Hmm. Actually, I do remember tearing it apart and crushing it with these very hands... and then Keith woke up, and then...?*

"Auuuggh!" I held my head as a weird sound escaped my lips. I could see the events that had just occurred replaying in my mind, in real time.

When Keith had opened his eyes, he'd called out to me in a feeble voice, and then for some reason, placed a hand on my cheek. That was fine and good. At least, up until that point.

But then, what happened after! Keith placed his lips against my cheek and then... he k-kissed me!!

In my confusion, I didn't know how to react, and could only stare blankly with my eyes wide. But then, Keith…! He looked at me with that pretty face of his, with an expression like he was ready to melt! And he just kept staring at me, just like that! Just thinking about it was enough to almost cause my head to explode.

And that sensation, too! I never thought that someone else's lips would be so soft. *Wasn't that my first kiss? Hmm? Wait… why does it feel like I've felt something like that before?*

In fact… is the feeling of someone else's lips really a first for me? Why does it feel like I've experienced this before? And… whose lips?

"…Katarina. Are you alright?"

A voice called out to me as I remained lost in my thoughts. I turned around, only to see Jeord standing behind me, with an expression of displeasure on his face.

"Y-Yes!" Still shaken, I managed to squeak out a response.

Jeord stepped forward, inspecting the now-sleeping Keith — the very same Keith who had just done something baffling, and then fallen asleep again.

"That was… quite the reaction, from what I could see. Perhaps a side effect of the magic being dispelled. He is most likely simply sleeping."

"I… see." I was so relieved that the magic had been dispelled. But what just happened was way too intense. I still couldn't get my thoughts together.

"However… even if he was half-awake, he really went and did it, I see." Jeord placed a hand on my chin.

In my confusion, all I could do was gape. *Could it be…?!* Just when I thought Jeord's face was a little too close for comfort, I felt that same soft sensation on my lips once more. The thing responsible, of course, was another person's lips.

With a soft sound, Jeord drew away. "A disinfectant, you see. You are mine after all, Katarina. I cannot simply overlook another man trying to snatch you away," Jeord said, sulking like a child.

I suddenly remembered everything that I had forgotten — all at once.

That's right... that kiss just now wasn't my first kiss. My first kiss was taken by Jeord a while ago... and on top of that, he even proposed to me, saying that he loves me!

I had forgotten about all that in the chaos of Keith's disappearance. But how could I have forgotten something like that...!

Then Jeord, who was still sulking childishly, said, "Hmm. It would seem that my feelings were not appropriately conveyed. Perhaps one kiss isn't enough? Then shall I do it again...?"

What terrifying words! I immediately shook my head. "No, I remember all of it! I'm fine, just fine," I replied, desperately.

Jeord seemed a little disappointed at my response. "Is that so... I see."

From there, my confusion continued to build. *What am I going to do? What am I supposed to do?* I was in a panic! *Jeord kissed me, said he loved me, and then... but then Keith, why did he...?* It was no good. There was simply too much at once.

Ugh, my face feels like it's on fire! My heart won't stop beating either! I can even hear it! Augh!

"Woof!"

And on top of all my confusion, a mysterious sound joined the fray. Of course.

"Woof woof."

I had no idea what was going on anymore. I couldn't grasp this situation at all. What was all this woofing during this tumultuous time?

...*Wait. What?!* The mystery sound came from very close to me. It obviously sounded like a puppy of some kind, but there shouldn't have been anything like that in this room.

Glancing toward the source of the sound, my eyes fell upon the remainders of the black snake, which I had compressed into a ball earlier. The sound had come from within that mass.

"...Huh? What?" I stared blankly at the black ball. It seemed to be... moving, forming itself into a new shape. *Is that snake thing back again?!* I steeled myself, and was ready for anything... but the new shape that the ball took was...

"...A puppy?"

Where the black mass once was now sat a black puppy — an adorable one, too.

"Wh-What?!" I could only guess that this puppy was formed from the black thing I'd torn off Keith! *Why is it a puppy now? One thing after another... nothing makes sense!*

Both Jeord and I seemed at a loss for words as we stared at the newly-materialized puppy. And then its eyes and mine met, and the puppy made a beeline for me.

Up until now, every single dog I had encountered in my life saw me as a mortal enemy. So I was prepared for anything... but then the puppy wagged its tail in joy as it approached me.

"Wh-Wha..." I could only stare on in shock.

Jeord's reaction was different from mine. "Are you alright, Katarina?!" he said, moving to peel the puppy off me.

"H-How cute...!" I said, hugging the puppy automatically.

"...Huh?" Jeord made a funny expression due to his surprise, but that didn't really register in my mind.

After all, I was incredibly moved! Ever since I was born — no, even in my previous life before this one, I had always been disliked by dogs. I loved animals, of course, including dogs, and I had no idea why they hated me. I was popular with the monkeys in the zoo and the mountains behind my home, for some reason, but dogs were always hostile toward me.

Petting a cute puppy this way made me feel like an ancient war had ended. Mutual enemies had finally put down their arms. Ah… I was finally able to feel a dog's soft fur. Hugging a puppy was really a dream come true. I had lived all these years, and a lifetime before, disliked by dogs. And now this day had arrived!

I continued ruffling the puppy's fur. It never once even bared its teeth at me. At long last, my dream had been fulfilled! I held the puppy tight, spoiling it in all the ways I could. The puppy seemed to enjoy this, if its rapidly wagging tail was anything to go by. *Ahh, so soft! So adorable.* It was like I was dreaming.

I could so easily lose myself in this newfound world, with my puppy, myself and… well, I guess it was just my puppy and me. Just as I was about to continue enjoying myself, mysterious laughter interrupted me.

"Hee hee…"

It was a clear voice, ringing out like a bell. I assumed that it was Jeord making a strange noise after being left out of the good time I was having with my puppy, but that was not the case. In fact, Jeord positioned himself before me and the puppy with his sword drawn and his expression grave.

He seemed to be glaring in the direction of the door. I followed his gaze, only to find a woman standing at the room's entrance. At a glance, she seemed to be a black-haired girl of around my age. The laughter probably came from her.

"What an interesting one you are… really," the black-haired girl said casually. It seemed like she was looking right past Jeord and his blade.

151

What a mysterious girl. Even though she seemed close to me in age, the way she laughed and smiled seemed almost childlike.

We continued to stare at the girl cautiously as she continued speaking. "But... after all that effort. I wanted to do a Dark Magic experiment and make a Dark Familiar, but I see that you've claimed it for yourself, hmm?"

"Dark... Familiar?" I repeated after her blankly, unable to understand.

"That puppy. I used the Dark Arts on your brother and made that Familiar. But I see you have dispelled that magic too."

"H-Huh?! This little thing here is a Dark Familiar? W-Wait! So you're the one who cast Dark Magic on Keith!"

"Why yes, that's me," the girl said, her expression not changing in the slightest.

How... How terrible! I couldn't believe that the perpetrator that Larna and the others had been looking for all this time would turn up on their own. From what Maria and Sora said, this person commanded immensely powerful Dark Magic. Would we be okay, facing such a foe?

I grew more uneasy, regarding the girl more cautiously than before. But she didn't seem to notice or care. "But then... how did you manage to take it for yourself? How mysterious... you don't have a drop of Dark Magic in you, from what I can see..." the girl mused, placing a hand on her cheek.

And then she suddenly asked, "Hey... tell me. Why? How?"

"Wha?! You ask me that, b-but..." I turned to look at the happy puppy, which was still wiggling in my arms.

Is this really true? This puppy is a Dark Familiar? I... guess it did come out of the black thing, yeah. But what is a Dark Familiar anyway? Is it dangerous? But it's so cute, I don't think it would hurt anyone...

"But, well... since you've taken it for yourself, there's not much to be done. Can't do much now, so... you can have that puppy."

"E-Eh...? Really? Thank you..." I thanked her reflexively, but... hmm? Something didn't feel right.

"Hee hee. You really are an interesting one, Katarina Claes..." the girl said, once again laughing in that same way.

"Wait... why do you know my name...?" There was no reason for her to know something like that.

Before I could ask, the girl moved. She raised an arm and muttered something under her breath. I saw Jeord raise his sword in response to her movements, but—

Before anything else could happen, the room was enveloped in an absolute, pitch-black darkness. It was a pure absence of light. I could not see a thing.

In the darkness, her voice echoed. "Honestly... I wanted to chat more, but I have to be going soon. We'll meet again somewhere, I'm sure..."

And with that, light suddenly returned to the room. But the girl was long gone.

"What... was that?" I muttered.

There was no response except for a single happy bark from the puppy cradled in my arms.

Immediately after the woman vanished, Larna and company rushed into the room. They had finally picked up on the trail of the perpetrator, and then felt a strong presence of dark magic, which eventually led them back to this very room. Jeord and I explained everything that had happened up until this point to Larna.

"Hmm. I see. And this is the Dark Familiar?" Larna asked, looking at the puppy in my arms. "There are many questions I would like to ask you, and in great detail. But we shouldn't stay here. Now that the Dark Magic cast upon Keith has been dispelled, we should go to a safe location immediately."

As she said, that was the best thing to do. So our little group started to exit the new-money mansion.

"...Um. Could we bring the little puppy with us?" It was simply too adorable. I couldn't just let it go. When I had set it down onto the ground and tried to leave, the puppy immediately plodded after me — it would break my heart to simply leave it in that room.

"Of course. It's definitely an interesting thing. And it doesn't pose any harm, from what I can see. Yes, we shall take it with us."

"Great! Thank you!" With Larna's permission, I scooped up the little black puppy and took it with us.

Perhaps because Keith was simply that tired, he remained fast asleep. He was terribly hurt all over, with injuries visible everywhere. But Maria helped heal his wounds with her Light Magic, and he at least looked a bit more like his old self now.

Our conversation shifted to the question of who should carry the injured and sleeping Keith.

"Ah, I have just the thing," Larna said. She withdrew a mat from the luggage pack Sora was carrying. It was the same one we'd had our picnics on.

Keith was laid gently on the mat, and Larna said something under her breath. Before I knew it, the mat had lifted a few centimeters off the ground.

"Wow! That's amazing!" I cheered, unable to contain my excitement.

Larna informed me that this was nothing more than a simple adaptation of the Wind Magic she specialized in. It was very much like a flying carpet of some kind. I asked enthusiastically if the mat would take to the skies and zip around freely in the air, but unfortunately it turned out that a few centimeters was the limit.

As I described my vision of a flying carpet to Larna, her eyes sparkled with delight. "I see... what a novel idea! Perhaps we could expand on that..." Maybe we would see a real flying carpet in the future!

With Keith now safely on the hovering mat and the black puppy cradled in my arms, we finally stepped out of the new-money mansion. There were hardly any guards on the way out. I asked Larna what that was all about, and was told that they had been dealt with while the three of them had been searching for the Wielder of Darkness. This really was the strongest party ever.

With that... my journey, and the search for Keith, was finally over.

Under the name Larna Smith, I hold a senior position at the Magical Ministry — though my real name is Susanna Randall.

I had just finished compiling a report detailing the Keith Claes kidnapping incident. With the report in hand, I decided to pay a visit to Jeffrey Stuart, the first prince of the kingdom, and technically my fiancé.

Jeffrey greeted me with his usual flippant smile. "Hey there. That all ended up being quite the ordeal, didn't it?"

"Yes, quite. It really went beyond my expectations, and not in a good way." Indeed, this particular case had ended up being a lot more trouble than I could have ever imagined. As for how it ended, Keith had been rescued, and the mansion and its owner had been seized by the Ministry.

We were still dealing with the aftermath. The staff assigned to the case had been working hard, especially my subordinate, Raphael. He had quite literally been working around the clock, hardly resting, if at all.

"Good work indeed! Well then, I helped out too, so let's hear all about the specifics."

"Sure. I owe you one, after all." By sharing what information I had with him, we were always able to plan for the worst. If and when the situation called for it, Jeffrey's power and status as a royal, combined with my capabilities as a high-ranking member of the Ministry, could be put to good use. So we often shared information with each other, unless it was incriminating or disadvantageous for one or the other of us to know about.

I started going over the specifics of the Keith Claes kidnapping case. Firstly, the main suspect who had currently been accused of the kidnapping and violent abuse of Keith was one Thomas Coleman — Keith's half-brother, born to a different mother. The son of Viscount Coleman and originally the heir to the family name, he had been raised without ever wanting for anything, and somewhere along the way became a useless, conceited man.

He was quite the troublemaker in the Coleman estate. Shortly after his social debut, there were reports of him kicking up trouble with other nobles. As a result of his behavior, Viscount Coleman decided that Thomas's younger brother should inherit his title instead. That caused Thomas to fly into a rage, and he soon started to get involved with ruffians and criminal elements, causing one outrageous scene after another. In the end, even Viscount Coleman himself could no longer cover for his wayward son, and had to resort to expelling him from the family estate.

With that being said, he wasn't simply kicked out the door — in fact, the viscount saw fit to grant Thomas a small home in the city, as well as provide him with a fair sum of coin. Given how spoiled he was and how he had lived most of his life, however, there was no way Thomas would keep quiet for long.

Indeed, he soon used up all of his money, and then turned toward extortion, causing no end of problems for those around him. Soon enough, no one would interact with Thomas in any way, shape, or form. That was when he coincidentally witnessed Keith in the city, and experienced a sharp pang of jealousy. These feelings caused him to fantasize about Keith's downfall, which was the root cause of the kidnapping.

But at that point, Thomas had neither coin nor status. How could he take his revenge, given that he had no allies of any kind…? The answer came in the form of a certain woman. According to Thomas's testimony, said woman approached him one day out of the blue. She bought him food and drinks, and listened to all he had to say enthusiastically — passionately, even. Thomas spoke of his jealousy and hatred toward Keith, and about his plans for his half-brother's downfall. That was when the mysterious woman offered to help.

Before he knew it, and without even lifting a finger, Thomas found himself in a mansion once more, living the elegant and opulent life that he craved. Although he had assumed that the mansion simply belonged to the woman in question, the reality was quite different. In truth, the woman had used Thomas's noble title and a fair sum of her own coin to temporarily rent the place.

As for the original inhabitants of the mansion, though they were certainly guilty of crimes and dark deeds, neither the servants nor their master knew a thing about the events that transpired in the house. They had been paid to act a certain way and do certain things, and they had followed those instructions unquestioningly. In fact, there was a high chance that the Dark Arts had been used on them — strongly suggesting that they should overlook any suspicious points, and not ask any questions. Given that there were many fuzzy points in their collective memories, this was highly likely.

Soon enough, the woman brought Keith from someplace, after which he was confined to a room and restrained. Thomas would commit acts of physical violence against the restrained Keith, claiming that he would soon become a slave and be sold to bidders in foreign lands.

Piecing together the various pieces of testimony I had received from eyewitnesses, it was plain to see that Thomas was hardly the mastermind behind all this. He was nothing more than a cowardly puppet, whose status and name had been used to commit this crime. The one truly responsible, surely, was the woman who had approached Thomas to begin with. She was none other than the Wielder of Darkness who had spirited Keith away in the first place. However...

"Well? Has she been captured yet? The mastermind."

"...Not yet." I furrowed my brow as I gave Jeffrey my response. She was a loose end that still eluded us.

"Oh ho. For someone as clever as you to let her slip away..."

"The enemy is every bit as clever, I assure you. I cannot find her location."

"So... you mean to say that we still don't know who she is, or where she is?"

"Well... I do have an idea. It's somewhat of a leap, but still..."

"Oh? So who is this mystery person that has caused so much trouble for you? Do tell."

"...If my assumptions are correct, the culprit is most likely someone from within the Dieke family."

"Marquess Dieke and company, right? The very same that Raphael testified against?"

"Indeed, yes. The family that stained their hands and got involved with Dark Magic quite some years ago."

"But didn't we round up everyone in that family who had anything to do with Dark Magic, even in the slightest?"

"So we thought, yes..." I proceeded to inform Jeffrey of the truths uncovered during this incident — secrets about the Dieke family.

The many crimes of the powerful and well-connected Dieke family had been brought to light thanks to Raphael's testimony. For their crimes directly involving the use of Dark Magic, Madam Dieke and all of her conspirators were arrested — at least, that was what we assumed.

However... there was more to it. Firstly, that woman, who introduced herself as Sarah to Thomas, knew a little too much about the Dark Arts; she knew of the existence of Familiars of darkness and how to craft them, and how to absorb and drain the essence of others to bolster her powers.

As I thought, this Sarah woman was by no means an incredibly powerful mage with bottomless reserves of Dark Magic. All she had been doing was draining energy from Thomas. Dark Magic was, after all, obtainable in exchange for a life. But the magic granted in such an exchange was finite, and could very well be used up over time.

However, there was a workaround. This was information that few within the Ministry knew of, but it was possible to replenish one's reserves of Dark Magic by absorbing energy from other people. "Energy" did not mean mana, or magic, or anything like that. Instead, the Wielder of Darkness drained the life force out of someone, and if that continued, the victim would die.

On top of all that, individuals bearing strong negative emotions supplied much more Dark Magic when drained. Putting the pieces together, it was fair to assume that Thomas's life force had been continuously drained from him over the course of this incident.

After we had arrested Thomas, we had done all we could for him. Although he recovered enough to be able to talk, he was exceedingly weak, and from the looks of it didn't have long to live. I did some research on Thomas and his activities up until this point, and from what I gathered, he had been healthy as a horse up until a while ago. Ministry staff who didn't know about the details of the incident could only scratch their heads at his sudden downturn.

This information about Dark Magic was only known to a select few. So why did that woman know of it? And then there was the case of Marquess David Mason, the perpetrator behind Katarina Claes's kidnapping. He, too, had received information on how to gain Dark Magic from the Dieke family.

However, he was only taught how to obtain it, not to adapt it or properly use it. The man knew nothing. In fact, the same was true within the Dieke family — even with its hands stained in the pursuit of Dark Magic, the specifics of certain techniques weren't widely known throughout the family.

As such, the fact that this Sarah woman knew so much about the Dark Arts and its intricacies was very suspicious. Perhaps she was also one of the individuals heavily involved in the research of Dark Magic in the Dieke family...

...Or so I thought. I decided to question our captives, and soon more new information about the Diekes was revealed. In their pursuit and research of the Dark Arts, the Diekes had granted a few specific people these powers, not just Raphael and the man who had possessed him. It was all part of Madam Dieke's contingency plan — should anything ever happen to Sirius (Raphael), there would be a Plan B.

The unwilling recipients for these dark powers were often orphans or slave children purchased or picked up from one source or another. Amongst them, many lost their lives when the ritual failed, and many more to the complications that followed even if the ritual did succeed. Though they prepared these children for future use, with the apparent success of Sirius's ritual, they became unnecessary.

Sirius was raised as planned, and the Dieke family could do whatever they wanted with these children.

Those that survived and successfully obtained Dark Magic ended up being used in the family's research. However, due to the twisted nature of the experiments that they were made to undergo, most of these survivors lost their minds — it was all too much to bear.

In the end, Raphael's testimony revealed all of the Dieke family's crimes. But those conducting the research feared that their sentences would be compounded if the Ministry learned of these experiments — so many of these children were disposed of before the truth of the matter was discovered. Amongst them there was a young girl with black hair who was particularly known for her high Dark Magic aptitude.

"That's pretty messed up. I see now that the twisted nature of the Dieke family went a lot further than I thought," Jeffrey said, frowning.

"Villains and scum, all of them. If I had not gone along this line of questioning, they would surely have all remained silent. Good thing they did talk — saved me a lot of trouble." They hadn't wanted to talk, of course, but with some persuasion and confronting them with evidence, they'd had no choice but to start talking.

"However, if your deductions ring true... this Sarah girl is also a victim of the Dieke family's deeds, isn't she? If what those scoundrels said is true, shouldn't she be dead, disposed of by their own hands? Is this Sarah truly the mastermind?"

"They say disposed, yes, but not with their own hands. They used the services of some crooks here and there, to hide bodies and the evidence. Shoddy work, most likely. There's a high chance that some of them could have survived. In addition, based on the information I extracted from Thomas and all those involved in the case, their descriptions match this woman. There's no mistaking it."

"Is that right? This mysterious girl from the Dieke family... what is her real name, then? Sarah would be nothing more than an alias, no?"

The furrow in my brow intensified at Jeffrey's question. "... About that. The girl never had a name to begin with. They were... assigned a number, you see."

Jeffrey's expression twisted into a look of disgust. I probably looked the same way. Yes, the origin of the girl named Sarah was far too cruel. She was a tragic victim of her circumstances. Her plight should be empathized with. However... that gave her no reason to impart this same hurt and pain unto others.

Why did Sara cause all this pain? Was it a sort of twisted retribution against Katarina and the others for bringing about the downfall of the Dieke family? Or was it just like the imprisoned researchers claimed — had she simply lost her mind, and committed crimes for her own amusement?

None of this would ever come to light as long as the girl remained on the loose. We knew who she was. All that was left was her location.

I organized my thoughts. It was time for the next report, which was about Katarina Claes, and a bizarre event that had happened during this case. From what I had heard, Katarina had freed her brother Keith who, at the time, was bound by the Dark Arts. He was to become a sacrifice for the creation of a Dark Familiar.

According to Jeord, this black mist (most likely the Familiar's incubational form) was torn apart by Katarina's bare hands. And then Katarina dealt the finishing blow to the scattered pieces of dark mist on the ground by crushing them, again with her bare hands.

Jeord then went on to describe how Katarina looked at the time — according to him, she looked very much like when she had finished off a snake that had wandered into her fields. For some reason, he had a faraway gaze in his eyes as he described the events.

First of all, what would a noble lady be doing in a field, disposing of snakes...? But anyway, to be able to simply crush that unknown black mass with her bare hands... Katarina Claes may be a much more impressive individual than I had initially assumed.

And then there was how Katarina herself worded it. *"I felt like I could do it, so I did!"* I couldn't help but start laughing. I laughed so hard I felt like I couldn't breathe. When he heard what had happened, Jeffrey started laughing too. I suppose we had the same sense of humor.

After a while he calmed down, still wheezing between breaths. It took a while for Jeffrey to finally finish. "In any case... why was Lady Katarina able to do that? She has no Light Magic, surely? Are you perhaps suggesting that she has control over the Dark Arts?"

"That was what I thought as well, but that doesn't make any sense. After some questioning, I discovered that it was most likely due to the influence of a magical tool that is attuned to Dark Magic."

"A Dark Magic tool, you say?"

I placed the object that Katarina had entrusted to me on Jeffrey's desk.

"Hmm. A mirror, I suppose?" Jeffrey wondered, taking the object into his hands and regarding it with a skeptical expression.

"Not exactly. Simply an ornament of some kind, it seems."

True, it did fit into a woman's hand easily, and it was relatively round. It did very much look like a mirror. Despite its round shape and borders, however, there was no mirror of any kind in it — a mysterious ornament, and that was that.

Honestly speaking, this rough and somewhat primitive ornament was not well designed. From what I had discovered, the item wasn't common in stores. If anything, it was a small knick-knack that one would find in an open-air stall. A small piece of scrap one could buy in a little corner of the city with some change. It was something that would never sell well.

"I couldn't tell just by looking at it, but Maria and Sora were able to sense traces of Dark Magic emanating from the object. I did some research, and from my observations, it would seem like this thing is similar to the magical tools I'm developing now."

"So, someone has been spying at the Ministry again, and emulating your work to make this tool?"

"Not exactly. I showed the round thing to someone who's well versed in the history of bone and porcelain crafts. From what they can tell, it's very old. It most likely existed back before Sorcié even became a kingdom — back when Dark Magic hadn't been declared taboo yet. And, as fate would have it, it eventually ended up at the shop that Katarina and the others visited."

"Oh ho, that is impressive indeed. Given that she was able to take hold of something like that so casually, Lady Katarina is really something else."

"Exactly. If it were me, I definitely would have looked right over it. Katarina has good instincts, at least for some things." The more I looked at the mystery ornament in Jeffrey's hands, the more I felt that to be true.

"So... Lady Katarina used this magical tool over here, and dispelled the Dark Magic cast on her brother?"

"That would seem to be the case. But there's one more thing... the Dark Familiar did materialize." Yes, the Familiar that the woman had been trying to extract from Keith had taken form.

"Oh? A Familiar really appeared?"

"Indeed. Katarina took a liking to it, and so she brought it back with her..."

"Hmm. So... is the Ministry currently investigating this Familiar?"

"Well... about that..."

"Go on, Pochi! Fetch!"

I threw the wooden stick into the distance, and the black puppy happily ran after it. Before long, he returned with the stick firmly in his mouth, his tail wagging fiercely as if to say "Praise me, praise me!" *Ahh, so cuuute!* I had fallen victim to Pochi's irresistible charm.

"Young miss, are you quite alright?" Anne asked, maintaining some distance from Pochi.

"Huh? What do you mean, Anne?"

"Don't you 'what do you mean, Anne?' me, young miss. After all, is that not the dog...?" Anne stopped short, not finishing her sentence.

"Ah, it's fine, no worries. Lady Larna said that there was no problem!"

"I... I see..."

Pochi's true origins had been explained to a handful of people close to me. Although he looked just like a cute puppy at first glance, he did have several unique abilities that made it difficult to hide what he was. This was probably why Anne, who was still not used to him, was afraid. *Even though he's so cute? Come on, Anne... Well, she'll come around to Pochi's charms eventually, I'm sure.*

The little puppy that we had brought back after the Keith rescue operation was more than just a dog. From what I was told, he was some kind of Familiar born of Dark Magic. He could be compared to a golem, like Keith's earth golems, though a more evolved version.

Pochi's body was full of Dark Magic, so he was originally seen as a dangerous creature, and was to be taken away by the Ministry to be investigated. But the puppy had become completely attached to me. Even if he were taken away, he would do everything he could to return to me — including transforming back into a cloud of black mist and flying home.

To ensure that he'd never be separated from me, Pochi decided to hide himself in my shadow. That way, no one would be able to take him from my side. Although the people from the Ministry had tried a bunch of different things to remove him, Pochi remained stubbornly stuck with me.

Lady Larna eventually gave up, saying, "This... is a lost cause. We should just have Katarina look after it and call it a day," with a tinge of regret in her voice. Just to be sure, they ran a series of tests on the puppy and me to ensure it wouldn't be a danger to me or anyone else. Once those tests were finished and I promised to bring Pochi over to the Ministry when requested, paperwork was signed and the black puppy officially became my pet.

I kept being surprised when the puppy dissolved into a cloud of mist or suddenly leapt into my shadow. But even so, he was my adorable puppy, and I loved him to bits.

Interestingly, Pochi didn't need to eat any kind of dog food. And he seemed very intelligent — he'd dissolve into my shadow and calmly wait if I asked him to. I didn't even need to build a dog house! What a convenient pet.

On top of all that, my position in the Ministry after graduating from the academy was pretty much a sure thing thanks to Pochi. I was even assigned a proper title! "Wielder of a Darkness Familiar."

Well, I guess I wasn't really doing anything useful except looking after the pup, but with this, I'd be able to hold my head high and walk through the Ministry's halls. I would also be able to hold off on getting married to Jeord and becoming royalty.

And so I named the puppy "Pochi" and gained a pet of my own.

"Whatever does 'Pochi' mean, young miss?" Anne had asked, confused.

"Isn't that the first name that comes to mind when you think of a dog?" I'd replied, but Anne didn't seem to get it. It was a common name for dogs in Japan, but apparently dogs in this world had naming trends of their own, and "Pochi" wasn't one of them. But I thought that naming the puppy that made him even cuter. In fact, he was so cute that I ended up playing with him daily in the manor's gardens.

I had returned to Claes Manor a while ago. Though we'd managed to rescue Keith from his kidnapper, he was still very weak and injured all over. So he was instructed to rest quietly at the manor for a while. I was worried about him, so I'd decided to move back home from the dormitories for now. Thankfully, lessons at the academy were already ending, so this didn't cause any problems.

But even though I'd declared that I wanted to look after Keith, I was quickly dismissed and chased out of the room. "With all due respect, young miss, you being here would inevitably increase our workload. Master Keith cannot possibly recuperate in such a noisy environment. It would be best for you to step outside," said one of our best servants.

...What a bummer. Come to think of it, I feel like the servants have become really strict with me lately. Even Anne! When I decided

to ask my friends about this, they all told me how gentle and accommodating their own servants were. I complained about this to Anne, only to learn the shocking truth — "You see, young miss... we have been specifically instructed by the Madam to be stricter with you."

Mother, how could you...?

And so it came to be that I, Katarina Claes, who had specifically moved back from the dormitories to spend time with Keith, ended up with nothing much to do. Instead, I spent most of my time playing with Pochi. Luckily, that was a lot of fun. Pochi would follow me around, wagging his tail.

As if reminded of something as she continued looking in our direction, Anne asked me a question. "A while ago, when you first departed with the people from the Ministry, young miss... I happened to see Lady Maria from a distance. There was something perched on her shoulder, unless I was mistaken. Was that a pet of some kind as well?"

"Hmm? Oh, that? That's a magical tool."

"A... magical tool?" Anne repeated after me blankly, evidently having never heard the term before. I gave Anne a brief explanation of the tool on Maria's shoulder, which was the Ugly Bear, Alexander.

"How impressive... to think that something like that could exist!" Anne did seem impressed.

I gave her a brief nod. "It's definitely something..." The bear had a terrible personality, but it had played an important part in the rescue operation. You could even say it played the most important part, since we would have never found Keith without the bear's help. I'd suppressed my dislike and formally thanked the bear for its assistance, only for the stupid thing to turn its nose up at me, ridiculing me again. I suppose, in the end, that bear and I would never see eye to eye.

After the trip had concluded, the bear was supposed to be sent to Prince Jeffrey as promised, but that had apparently become impossible, since it had become very attached to Maria over the journey. The bear refused to stay with the prince, behaving just like Pochi did. In the end, after its many struggles to return to Maria's side, Alexander the Ugly Bear was permanently assigned to Maria instead. Something else indeed.

On another subject, Lady Larna herself had received more materials and funding from Prince Jeffrey for a new search-and-track magical tool. She was overjoyed. "A new project, a new project!" she'd gushed, bouncing out of the office. Prince Jeffrey, who had been basically dumped by the bear, seemed to be feeling pretty down about the situation.

And so Alexander the Ugly Bear was now officially Maria's pet. I knew that meant that I'd have to see the bear again whenever I met with Maria in the future. Just thinking about it made me feel kinda depressed.

If that bear was going to be with Maria from here on out, I had to do something to make sure we got along next time we met. *But… what could I do? Maybe I should give it a present? But what would a bear even like?*

As I continued thinking about a possible strategy for bear peace, a servant came running up from the direction of the manor, looking flustered. "Young miss, it's Master Keith…"

"What?! What happened to Keith?!" *What could it be?*

"…He has safely woken from his slumber," the servant finished, smiling.

Although we had arranged for a doctor to tend to Keith on-site as soon as we had returned, his body was significantly weakened from his ordeal. He had used up more than his usual share of stamina and had been sleeping ever since. He would wake up sometimes, and we would exchange a few words. Even so, it seemed like he was in a bit of a daze, and he'd immediately fall back asleep. Things continued that way for a while.

According to the doctor, Keith's body had recovered and he would surely wake up sometime soon. All we could do was wait.

"...I see. So he's awake at last..." I heaved a sigh of relief. Although I was told that he'd be fine, I couldn't help but worry at the fact that Keith remained asleep for all that time. "Well then, let's go see Keith. Ah, he'll probably be surprised if he suddenly sees you, Pochi. Go home for now, okay?"

With a prompt bark, the intelligent Pochi was soon snugly tucked away in my shadow. With my preparations complete, I headed toward where my beloved brother lay — having opened his eyes for the first time in days.

When I entered the room, I found Keith, who had been lying down all this time, sitting up in bed. His blue eyes were now fully open, and immediately focused on me as I went inside.

"Keith!" I bounded happily to Keith's bedside and hugged him tight. "Keith! I'm so glad you're alright... so glad..." I said, sniffling in between words as I held him.

"Big Sister... I do apologize for causing you to worry so. I would also like to thank you. For saving me," Keith said, smiling faintly, his eyes brimming over with tears just like mine.

Then I started explaining what had happened on our journey to Keith, going over all the details from beginning to end. After all, he had been asleep all this time and wouldn't know anything that had happened. But he did apparently vaguely recall the moment of his rescue.

As I continued hugging him, I told Keith about everything. About how Lady Larna, Prince Jeord, Sora, Maria, and I had set off in search of him, using the bear-shaped tool. Keith seemed very interested in the tale, although he seemed unsettled by what he heard at times. Nevertheless, he continued listening.

Eventually, the story moved to the point where we had found the new-money mansion. When I told Keith of how I had grabbed the swirling dark mist with my bare hands, he couldn't contain his surprise. "...Big Sister. No matter the situation, that was clearly reckless," he said, troubled.

"B-But...! I needed to get that mist out of the way for you to finally wake up!" Now that I was retelling the story, I started recalling that specific point in time. After I had peeled the dark mist off him, Keith, for some reason...

Before I knew it, I had let go of him, and was now a few steps away. Keith looked at me, surprised. "What is it, Big Sister...?"

"Um... well. You see... when you woke up at the mansion, it seemed like you were sleep-walking...? Or sleep-talking..." Yes — it was exactly that. Keith had definitely been half-asleep. That was why he had said something about a "dream." I think Keith had just confused me with someone he liked.

But... should I even bring that up? He doesn't seem to remember. I decided we should just bury those memories back in the darkness.

As Keith stared at my still-flustered self, he seemed to be momentarily lost in thought, and then — "I... sleepwalking. Huh?! Y-You mean to tell me that... that was not a dream?!" Apparently he had remembered everything. All the color drained from his face.

Oh no! I quickly tried to reassure him. "Um... you were half-asleep, and pretty dazed, so there was no helping it. You confused me for someone you like, right? It happens. But it's fine! I've already forgotten about it. You can forget all about it too, Keith."

"It happens"? Even I had a hard time convincing myself of that. But it had been said, and that was that. I looked earnestly at Keith, my face completely flushed.

"Forget…? All about it…?" Keith muttered.

"Y-Yes! Exactly. Let's do that." *Yes, that's for the best.* If word got out that Keith had mistaken his adoptive sister for his lover and kissed her, it wouldn't be good for his reputation. He would surely agree that this should be stuffed down the memory hole. Or so I thought…

"I refuse."

"…Wha?"

Keith turned to me with a serious expression. "I refuse to forget about it. Nor will I pretend it never happened."

"Keith…?"

Although I was some distance away from Keith, he was soon by my side. His blue eyes focused straight on me. "Perhaps I was indeed sleep-talking. But it was my first kiss, with the person I love. There is no possible way I could forget about something like that."

"Huh? Um… what do you mean, Keith?" His first kiss, with the person he loved? If I followed that line of reasoning, the person Keith loved had to be…

"Ever since I was a child, Big Sister… no. Katarina… I've liked you. As a woman. I… love you," Keith said, his face completely red.

What? Umm. Let me process this. So I am the person Keith loves…?

Hmm… well, I do love Keith too, he is very important to me. But, huh…? Did he say… "as a woman"? And that… he loves me? But that's…

173

With that, I finally pieced together the jigsaw in my head. I felt my cheeks rapidly heating up. My heartbeat was violently increasing. "Huh? Ah. Uh…" I was at a complete loss for words. The only sounds to escape my lips were strange single syllables, uttered at the red-faced Keith.

And then, all of a sudden… a whole flock of people invaded this space.

"Keith, whatever do you think you're doing? Confessing off the cuff? Katarina belongs to me."

"I would ask that very same question of you, Prince Jeord! Whatever are you saying? Lady Katarina belongs to no one!"

"Yeah, Mary's right. She doesn't belong to you."

"That's right… Lady Katarina does not belong to anyone! Ah, Lady Katarina… I've brought some novels I highly recommend… perhaps you would enjoy them, too."

"Sophia, Keith is the one who is ill, not Katarina. Perhaps your choice of get-well-soon gift is a little strange."

"Ah… Well, I baked some treats, perhaps Master Keith would enjoy them?"

How long had they been waiting there? Suddenly, all the regular suspects had rushed into the room.

Jeord was soon by my side, faster than my eyes could see. He wrapped his arms around me, as if to separate me from Keith. "Katarina is mine, yes?" he whispered, softly but clearly into my ears.

My cheeks were at critical mass. My heartbeat was so loud, I felt like I would explode! I didn't spend much time in Jeord's arms, though, as Keith was soon trying to retrieve me from his clutches.

"That won't do. I will not hand her over to you, Prince Jeord."

"Oh? I see that you have finally learned to speak up, Keith…" Jeord said.

The two of them now glaring daggers at each other — with me sandwiched in between. *Ugh! What was even going on? I don't know anymore!*

Maybe it was because I was in a panic, or maybe it was because the room had become so lively… or it may even have been in response to the strange sounds I'd made earlier. Before I knew it, Pochi had leapt out of my shadow, and was soon busy running circles around me and my friends. Between laps, he would stare at Alexander the bear, who was currently perched on Maria's shoulder.

All I could do was stare at this portrait of chaos, with my jaw hanging open in a daze. It was then that I heard a familiar voice…

"Cleared the Keith Claes route, huh! One on each arm, hmm?"

It was as if, in my ear, I could hear the voice of my best friend from my previous life.

~The Frustrations of Mary Hunt~

Having finally finished organizing the stacks of paperwork, I slammed the pile down on my table with a flourish and sighed deeply. This was work that I could have very easily finished in the blink of an eye under normal circumstances. I was unable to set my mind to it, however, and so it took quite a while.

With this, my work was finally finished, and I returned to my quarters at the academy's dormitories. Work, life, it was all the same. I just couldn't focus.

It had been like this for the past few days. I knew the reason full well, of course. It was simple, really — Katarina and her group had left in search of Keith… and I was not permitted to join them on their trip.

Katarina Claes was a very special person to me. She was very important in my life. When I had closed myself off from the outside world as a child in response to my stepsisters' cruel bullying, it was she who had saved me.

I did not have a shred of self-confidence then — it was Katarina who inspired me, and allowed me to live with my head held high. Whenever I faltered, it was she who extended her hand toward me. To not love someone like that was all but impossible.

Before I knew it, Katarina had become the most important person to me, deep in my heart. That was why I wanted to be by her side. In order to be with her, always, I worked hard in various ways.

However, Katarina was simply overflowing with charm. There were many others in her life. The tip of the spear, if I could describe it as such, was Katarina's current fiancé, prince Jeord Stuart. The prince was a genius — he was capable of anything, and had eventually become fond of Katarina. He employed any means necessary to ensure that she fell into his hands.

Although Jeord looked like any other dashing youth, I knew that he was quite the villain on the inside. Using his standing as Katarina's fiancé, Jeord had planned to immediately take her hand in marriage after her graduation from the Academy of Magic. As much as I hated the idea, I could predict that this was what the prince would do. After all, we had similar ways of thinking.

However... Katarina was, how do I put this — extremely dense. She did not notice any of Prince Jeord's advances, of course. If anything, my efforts over the years had paid off. I told Katarina at every opportunity that "becoming a royal was most tiresome." As a result, she was hardly eager about the entire marriage affair.

With the assistance of my allies, who were all also rather fond of Katarina, we planned to have her somehow cancel her engagement with the prince. To this end, we were deliberating a possible solution when...

After a complicated incident that caused much ado a short while ago, there was an unexpected development: Katarina, who was quite possibly the most dense person in the entire Kingdom of Sorcié, suddenly became aware of Prince Jeord's feelings toward her.

Riding on that success, Jeord began aggressively escalating his advances at a pace I had never seen before. While the rest of the council attempted to shield Katarina from his attempts, Jeord was quick to pile extra work on us. So despite our best efforts at interrupting his plans, Jeord managed to give us the slip time and time again.

And amidst all this, Katarina and Jeord left together on a trip, of all things! The reason was that Katarina's adopted brother, Keith Claes, had seemingly run away from home. He had returned to Claes Manor during a holiday period when he had suddenly gone missing. Shortly after a letter arrived addressed to the Claes family, claiming that Keith had left home of his own volition.

This was unnatural on numerous counts. Why would Keith, who loved Katarina so, suddenly choose to leave her side...? Many others thought the exact same, I'm sure, but there was little a young girl like me could do.

It was not like Katarina, however, to think that way. Before I knew it, she had declared that she would go on a journey to find her brother. In the most straightforward way, too! *"Keith surely ran away from home because I caused him too much trouble!"* she'd said.

In that case, I would accompany her too...! Or so I thought. Unfortunately, there were more complex circumstances at play, and I was unable to join Katarina on her journey. This was a tragedy in and of itself, but there was an even bigger problem: Jeord would be accompanying her!

Given that his approaches toward Katarina had been rapidly intensifying over the past few days, and he would be together with her the entire time, who knows what would happen. I was incredibly worried, to put it lightly.

Yet Katarina had become transfixed with the issue of Keith's disappearance, and had apparently all but forgotten about Jeord's advances, for now, at least. Try as he might, Katarina was no longer receptive to Jeord's efforts. A good thing indeed, but...

Just in case, I entered a formal request via the Ministry for another member of her journeying party to keep an eye on Jeord, so as to ensure that he would not unduly approach Katarina. Even so, this was the prince we were dealing with. I could never quite read his hand.

Ahh... if only I, too, could follow her on this journey! I was worried. Terribly worried, and also greatly displeased that I had been left behind.

Ever since Katarina had left, these feelings inside me had been swirling uncontrollably. In fact, they were getting in the way of my work at the council, and even preventing me from living well!

Ugh...! Just how long will it be until Katarina returns? Is she safe? I wondered, pacing meaninglessly in my quarters. My usual image of the infallible noble lady of high society had crumbled. I did not look anything like that now.

As I continued to pace around my room in pointless circles, I heard a knock on the door — a guest had arrived for me, according to my servant.

The one who had showed up was my current fiancé, prince Alan Stuart. He might have been Jeord's twin, but the two were nothing alike in terms of personality. The most striking difference was that Alan was... honest. A less flattering word to use might be "simple," or perhaps even a little childish at times. He was also among the many who were fond of Katarina.

Alan had actually only noticed his feelings for her just a year prior. He was dense too, though nothing near Katarina's level.

Although everyone around him knew that he had feelings for her ever since he was a child, it would seem that he himself hadn't noticed the entire time.

I suppose it was I who was responsible for that. I had done everything in my power to ensure that Alan would not notice how he felt about her. Why would I do such a thing? Well, it was to reduce the number of rivals competing with me for Katarina's hand, of course. It was nothing as sappy as, *"Oh, because Alan is my fiancé."* Do not misunderstand, I am somewhat fond of Alan. But Katarina will always come first.

When he finally noticed his feelings for Katarina, Alan turned to me, so trusting, and said, "There's someone else I like. Maybe my feelings will never reach her, but I can't lie to you. That's dishonest. We should cancel our engagement."

Truly, I was stunned at how honest Alan could be. In fact, I could not help but be worried about his future, given that noble society was swirling with snakes and other dark elements. Alan claimed that he could not tell me who this mystery person was. All I could do was think to myself, *But everyone already knows!*

However, my answer at the time was a firm "no." After all, if my engagement with Alan was called off, I would almost certainly be immediately engaged to someone else. And if that happened, it was likely that I could be married off on the spot. Perhaps it would come across as me tooting my own horn, but as a result of my countless years of hard work, I had quite the reputation as a refined lady in noble society. I was most popular indeed.

Honestly speaking, I would greatly abhor being married off to some man I did not know. I didn't think I could endure being apart from her. A compromise I could make was to be by Katarina's side, even if it would only be for a while.

My life goal was to spend the rest of my life with Katarina. This was no time for me, Mary Hunt, to go off getting married to men I didn't even know! That was why I also told Alan that there was someone else I loved, and that this person may never answer my feelings either.

"But… I will not give up! The possibility of it is low, yes, but I would like to at least try. So… I would greatly prefer it if you stayed, Prince Alan. After all, you are in a similar situation — you would be much more preferable to a new fiancé I did not know. So please, let us keep the engagement intact for now," I said, with tears in my eyes.

Alan, being the dense prince he was — and one of my rivals, no less — was quick to agree, without even a single hint of suspicion. "I get it. Until you and that person end up together… I'll continue being your fiancé."

I did feel bad for him, but at least now we shared a common goal! I pulled Alan into our little alliance, and plotted to nullify all of Jeord's aggressive approaches. But this time, he undoubtedly had the upper hand. Now that Katarina was out of my reach… would Jeord do something to her? I could not get that thought out of my mind.

Despite my obvious frustration and my markedly different behavior as of late, Alan still managed to hand me a letter — although he did seem somewhat cowed by my fury.

"A letter's arrived addressed to the council. Thought I'd bring it to you," he said, offering the letter to me.

"A letter, you say? From whom, exactly?" But upon taking a peek at it, I noticed a word that I loved dearly written there.

"Yeah. From Katarina, about her journ— hey!"

Before Alan could finish his sentence, I snatched the letter out of his hands and immediately set about reading its contents. Written in the letter was nothing to be alarmed about. It was simply Katarina happily describing the highlights of her trip in a relaxed manner.

The letter put me at ease. I sighed deeply once again, in spite of myself — this time in relief.

"H-Hey. Mary... I can read it too, right?" For some reason, Alan seemed terrified.

"But of course!" I replied, handing the letter over to the prince with a ladylike smile.

~The Worries of Alan Stuart~

My fiancée, Mary, had been weird lately. Guess you could say she's distracted — like her mind is on someone else. She keeps getting a grave expression on her face. The reason is probably — or well, definitely, the fact that Katarina had left on a trip.

Katarina Claes was my twin brother Jeord's fiancée, and me and Mary's close friend. The only daughter of Duke Claes was kind of a weirdo in many ways. But I liked how straightforward she was.

Mary was really attached to Katarina, ever since they were kids, and they were still good friends. That's why she was lonely now, because she got left behind.

Well, I didn't feel great about having to stay either. After all, I thought about Katarina as much as Mary did. But then, I guess my feelings for Katarina weren't quite the same. Mary just admired Katarina, and that was that. But for me, I loved her as a woman, even though she was my brother's fiancée.

But I'm dense. Even I know that. I only noticed these feelings last year, when Katarina was almost killed. I was surprised when I found out, but when I did, everything suddenly made sense.

But I couldn't just go and snatch away my brother's fiancée just because of my feelings. Everyone knew it was a political marriage, so maybe I'd be able to do it if they didn't get along. But look at Jeord — parading around pampering Katarina whenever he could.

I decided to lock my feelings away deep in my heart. But having thoughts about another girl like that wasn't fair to my fiancée, Mary. It was dishonorable. I couldn't just tell her who I liked, obviously, but I told her about my feelings.

I figured that Mary would be happy to call off the engagement, but then she said something totally out of the blue. She said that she liked someone else too, and that she couldn't talk to them either. She was in the same boat as me, with some kind of forbidden love.

Come to think of it, the place I saw Mary the most was at Katarina's manor. There was always a distance between us, and it seemed like Mary didn't really like me that much. But I was surprised that she had feelings for someone else this entire time.

If she canceled the engagement with me, she'd just be married off to someone else immediately, she said. So we decided to keep the engagement intact. It had been a year since then, and I still had no idea who the mystery person that Mary liked was.

Mary seemed to be working hard. With my position, there wasn't much I could do about my secret love. But seeing Mary give it her all made me hope that she and the person she liked would find happiness. Now that we'd both told each other about our feelings, I felt fonder of Mary, who'd just been my fiancée in name.

With that lovely face of hers, she'd declared, "I do not want for my dear friend, Katarina, to be monopolized by Jeord!" and asked me to tell her about what Jeord was up to. Well, I didn't want Jeord to do that either. Though the way Mary went about it felt like she was trying to get between the two of them.

Maybe because of what we were trying to do, Jeord and Katarina's relationship didn't really go anywhere. Jeord was always approaching her, but she was too much of a blockhead to notice his feelings.

But then, not long after she was rescued after being kidnapped, Katarina finally realized what was going on. Like this was some kind of trigger, Jeord's advances got way more intense. And then after that, this trip happened. Katarina's brother, Keith, apparently ran away from home. She went off to look for him, and Jeord went with her... which made me worried.

Mary wasn't just feeling sad because she was lonely. She was probably worried about Katarina being taken away from her forever, and that's why she was acting so weird. Honestly I was feeling the same way. I said I'd hide my feelings, but the more I thought about it, the more I was upset when I thought about Katarina marrying Jeord and becoming his... well, I didn't want to think about it. Guess I'm selfish in some ways after all.

I really hope nothing happens between them while they're gone, I thought as I finished up the rest of the work in the council chambers. With Jeord gone, our workload was a lot heavier. But I couldn't stop thinking about the traveling group, wondering where they were and what they were doing. I couldn't keep my mind on my work, so I ended up staying here late recently.

The sun was setting. *Time to get back to the dorm,* I was thinking, when a letter arrived. "To everyone at the student council," it said.

It was definitely written by her. I wanted to read it right then, but if it was something to do with something happening between Katarina and Jeord, I didn't want to think about it. So I hesitated before opening it. *Well, I guess I should let Mary know first anyway.*

Making up my mind, I cleaned up the place and headed back to the dorms. When I got to Mary's room, I saw that she was looking pissed off again.

"A letter's arrived addressed to the council. Thought I'd bring it to you," I said, showing Mary the letter.

"A letter, you say? From whom, exactly?"

"Yeah. From Katarina, about her journ— hey!"

Before I could even finish, Mary violently snatched the letter out of my hands. Unlike me, she didn't hesitate at all. She ripped the letter open and read it all quickly with the same look on her face.

Then her expression softened and she sighed deeply. Seemed like nothing bad was written in it, at least. She looked a lot more relaxed now, but she still had an edge in her expression. It was hard to deal with her when she was like this. But even so...

"H-Hey. Mary... I can read it too, right?"

She replied with one of her ladylike smiles, apparently not upset anymore. "But of course!" she said, handing me the letter.

I read it, and found that it was just Katarina happily describing her journey, and that was that. All's well that ends well, huh.

Relieved, I handed the letter back to her. The anxiety in my mind seemed to calm a little. Since the letter was addressed to everyone in the council, I guessed Sophia would be the next one to read it. I said this to Mary, who had already gone back to her usual self.

With a small smile, she said, "Indeed. I shall deliver it to her personally."

~The Melancholy of Sophia Ascart~

"Haaah…" *How many times have I sighed like this today? I've lost count…*

I returned to the dormitories as the sun began to set. I even picked up a book I had been interested in as of late in an attempt to cheer myself up, but I… just couldn't concentrate.

If I were to even get slightly absorbed in the book's contents, my mind would wander back to Katarina. *Is she alright?* I would think. No matter the book before me, even if it was one of my favorites… they simply could not win against the existence that was Katarina.

Katarina Claes… a dear friend of mine ever since childhood. We were friends even now. She was someone most important to me. I had first met her when I was ten, at a tea party held at the royal castle. I was born looking somewhat different than the people around me… and they would always stare at me as if I were some sort of curiosity.

I had locked myself away in my heart… but Katarina smiled at me. And then, she told me that I was beautiful, despite the fact that I hated how I looked, and how I was stared at because of it. I found salvation in Katarina's words… and was finally able to become someone new. In fact, I was only where I stood now because I had met Katarina, all that time ago.

And now, that very same person, who meant so much to me… had left on a journey. Katarina's adopted brother, Keith, had run away from home. She had left in search of him.

The disappearance of Duke Claes's son was not something to be taken lightly. It could not be made public, and only a small number of people could be involved in the search… I knew from the very beginning that this was no normal disappearance.

I was not strong, unlike Jeord or Maria. I wielded no power of any kind... even if I were to follow, I would only get in their way. Even I knew that much. However... understanding it logically was one thing. Coming to terms with my feelings... was another.

I had wanted to go, too... and my heart was filled with swirling emotions because I could not accompany her. And then there was another point of concern... Maria was fine, but to think that Jeord would follow her on this journey...

I mean Jeord Stuart, of course. Third prince of the kingdom, and Katarina's fiancé. When I first met Katarina she was already engaged to him, and he had always stuck close to Katarina back then, too. Although I sometimes felt like he was a little mean or mischievous... I understood that Jeord wasn't a bad person.

But... to just take Katarina all for himself! I could not agree with that! I could recall the numerous occasions in my childhood when I felt frustrated at Jeord for doing just that. And then... from what I heard, he intended to take Katarina's hand in marriage immediately after her graduation from the academy! If that really came to pass, Katarina would become fully monopolized by Jeord...

No! I won't accept that, I just won't! I have to do something to... interfere! With those thoughts in mind, I formed an alliance with Mary, who felt the same way, and we did everything in our power to foil Jeord's plans.

Maybe it was because of all our hard work...? Katarina had never noticed Jeord's feelings toward her all this time... but it would appear that she had recently come to understand. With that, Jeord's attempts at expressing his feelings greatly increased in intensity and frequency... and it was a most difficult time...

To leave together on a journey now, of all times! If anything happened between Jeord and Katarina on this trip... if Jeord really took her hand in marriage, then I would never be able to see her again! Ugh, that was unacceptable, just unacceptable! I could not find it in myself to give Jeord my blessing!

After all, my heartfelt wish was for Katarina to become my sister-in-law! If that were to happen, I would be able to live with her forever. For that to happen, I'd really like Big Brother to work a little harder... ah. About Big Brother...

My older brother, Nicol, was a most beautiful person! Not only that, he was sensitive, considerate, and gentle. Anyone would be proud to have him as an older brother. Due to his beautiful looks and peculiar aura, Big Brother was very popular with people of any gender. However, I also knew that he always had feelings for Katarina.

And yet...! Big Brother simply would not approach Katarina in any way! After all, if Nicol would really put his mind to it, anyone and everyone would fall prey to his charms! Yes, even Katarina! She would become all but entranced, too! No matter how much I told my brother to work harder, he would only shake his head... and say what he usually did. *"It would be most inappropriate. She already has a fiancé."*

Despite my brother's alluring looks and charms, he was actually a very straight-laced, serious, and somewhat rigid person on the inside. To begin with, what was all that about her "already having a fiancé"? Perhaps that was true for Jeord, but Katarina hardly saw him in that light. To me, this was the perfect opportunity, the best chance!

Katarina was straightforward, gentle and kind to everyone... everyone liked her, of course! She herself, however, did not seem aware of this in the slightest. Even Jeord, who had been ferociously attempting to woo Katarina ever since they were both children, never did get his feelings for her noticed.

"I'm only Prince Jeord's fiancée in order to fend off other women!" Katarina would always say such things. Any normal person would think this is impossible. Certainly, only Katarina would seriously declare something like that.

Katarina also really loved romance novels. That was how we came to know each other, after all. She would always read many wonderful stories about love and romance, and we would often get into passionate discussions. *"The knight in this story is so charming! Ah, that prince, too, I could fall for him in a heartbeat!"* Katarina would say.

However, when it came to discussions about our real lives... *"Well, I don't really have much luck with love and all that, you know?"* she'd say, much to the surprise of everyone around her.

I once asked her why, only for her to say, *"Well, I'm just a villainess at the end of the day, right?"* I could not understand what she meant at all.

In any case, it became clear to me that Katarina was, for some inexplicable reason, firmly rooted in the belief that she was not fated to experience matters of love, romance, and the like. Though now things were different, since she had noticed Jeord's feelings toward her.

However, Katarina's mind was filled with thoughts of Keith right before they set off. It even seemed like she had all but forgotten about noticing Jeord's feelings before... but there was the risk of her remembering everything if they traveled together for all that time! If that happened...

Ugh, I could feel those emotions swirling around inside me again. I simply could not stay still, and I soon found myself idling around in my room. After all, Mary did say, *"This is Prince Jeord we're talking about. Swift moves are to be expected."* If... If anything were to happen to Katarina during that trip...!

Perhaps it was because I had read a few too many romance novels up until this point... I could not stop my imagination from running wild. If anything, I could feel it all slowly getting worse.

A scene from a recent novel I had read comes to mind... of one knight of the princess's royal guard, proposing to the very same princess he served right before their journey reached an end. At night, the princess was unable to fall asleep no matter how hard she tried, and so she wandered outside her room... A drunk accosted the princess, and she was saved by that same knight. The princess would then fall for the knight, and their bond would deepen over the course of their journey.

However... once that journey was over, the two would never be able to meet again. She made up her mind — she would become bonded to the knight before returning to the royal castle, and on a night close to the journey's end, she made her way to where the knight stood...

"...Nooooooooooo! You mustn't!!" I screamed, envisioning Katarina as the princess, and Jeord as her knight. As I did so...

"I do not know what it is that one mustn't do, Sophia. However, the sun has set. Avoid raising your voice in the dormitories." A somewhat exasperated voice came from behind me — I turned around quickly, only to see my brother Nicol.

"B-Big Brother!? Why are you here...?"

For some reason, he had a most exasperated expression on his face. "To deliver something the council has requested of me. Work, of course. I thought to visit you as well, Sophia, and so came to the dormitories. You would not respond no matter how many times I called out to you. You would do well to... address your daydreaming tendencies."

"A-Ah… my apologies…" Big Brother's stern warning caused me to inadvertently withdraw into myself. It was as he said, though… I did have a habit of daydreaming. I would get lost in countless fantasy worlds in my mind. I myself hardly noticed, of course… but sometimes I really did become unaware of my surroundings in the process. I… had to be a little more careful.

Big Brother's expression softened upon seeing my embarrassment. Perhaps he was being considerate. "Tell me, Sophia. Why were you pacing in irregular circles, alone in your room?" he asked.

It would seem that he was worried about me… Big Brother really was a gentle person. I told him about everything — about how lonely I was after Katarina departed on her trip, and how I was worried that she was together with Jeord.

"I understand you being lonely due to Katarina's journey. However, Katarina is Jeord's fiancé. Is their bond deepening not a good thing?"

Although my brother responded in such an orthodox fashion, his words did not match up with his expression. Many would say that Big Brother's expression hardly changed, if at all. I, however, knew better — I was his little sister, after all, and he could not fool my eyes. While what Nicol said was right… he could not hide his expression of sorrow.

"Come now, Big Brother, you're worried as well, aren't you? You're only putting up a brave front… you should really be more honest with yourself!" I said.

"What are you talking about, Sophia?" he replied, all the while with a somewhat difficult look about him.

Just as I was about to start a back-and-forth with my stubborn brother, a visitor showed up at the door. It was Mary — one of my close friends, and another member of the student council. She had brought us a letter from Katarina.

Written in it were Katarina's observations on her journey, and the sights and sounds she experienced. There was not a single word about Jeord — I suppose nothing had happened between them.

I heaved a deep sigh of relief, before glancing sideways at my brother. As I expected, he, too, seemed relieved by these developments. *Sigh...* He really wasn't very honest with himself, sometimes.

~The Troubles of Nicol Ascart~

The reason I decided to assist Jeord in his absence was a simple one. He was my childhood friend, and I had agreed to assist the student council with some of its affairs, because the council's members were each becoming very unwell.

Unwell though they might be, they were by no means ill. They were all simply very depressed, or collectively had something on their minds. As such, they were unable to focus on their work.

I knew of the cause. Katarina, whom I adore, had left on a journey — without them in her company. However, she did not do this for fun. She had only left on a journey due to the sudden disappearance of her brother, Keith. She had departed in search of him.

The sudden disappearance of Duke Claes's son was a sensitive matter. It could not simply be made public. Even if a smaller party made the search more difficult, a large group could not be dispatched without attracting attention.

In addition, those left behind were all members of the student council. They had tasks of their own, especially now that the graduation ceremony was this close. It would not be acceptable for seniors such as them to suddenly drop all their responsibilities and leave the academy.

This was why Katarina had no choice but to depart with a small group of companions. Those left behind knew this fact as well. Even so, they found it difficult to keep calm in the face of these developments. The existence of Katarina served as their motivation... She was a special person to many. That much I understood well.

Yes. I, Nicol Ascart, thought of Katarina as a special individual, as well. I first met her when I was accompanying my sister on her visit to Claes Manor. Meeting Katarina was a salvation of sorts for Sophia — and for that I am eternally grateful. However... before I knew it, I, too, was a slave to Katarina's charms.

Although people claim that I have a certain charm that draws people to me, I feel that such a statement would be best reserved for Katarina. After all, I find myself impossibly attracted to the person known as Katarina Claes.

However, she already had an official fiancé during our first meeting. She was engaged to none other than my childhood friend, Jeord Stuart, the third prince of the kingdom. I had not seen Jeord for a while. When we crossed paths once more, he had completely changed — he had completely fallen for Katarina.

A noble lady who was officially engaged to my childhood friend. If it were a political marriage, perhaps... but Jeord really loved her. To even think of pulling the two apart — unforgivable. There was nothing I could do. Nothing but suppress the feelings I had for Katarina with all my might.

I had to do this. I had no choice but to do this, I told myself. Sophia, however, had found out about my feelings, and often tried to spur me on. Sophia was fond of Katarina, as I was. She believed that she would be with Katarina forever if the two of us were wed.

While Sophia was a gentle and good girl, she had a tendency to daydream. She often gave in to her overactive imagination. In the past, that was all she used to do — dream. Perhaps it was due to the influence of her friends, but Sophia had recently taken to actually putting her plans into action. It is something I should be glad about. However, her efforts to unite Katarina and myself were most troubling.

One such incident occurred a while ago, at the school festival. Sophia insisted that Katarina and I should play the role of lovers, re-enacting part of a play. I performed quite poorly then. Katarina, who had accepted her role without hesitation, whispered into my ears words of love. I had to deliver similar lines too. Under normal circumstances my logical reasoning would hold me in check, but my emotions got the better of me.

Before I realized it, I was holding Katarina's body in my arms. I never wanted to let go.

Soon enough, I regained control of my faculties, and quickly released her. However, the burning flame in my heart did not cool for quite a time. In truth, I knew. It was not the fault of my sister, even if she did spur us on. The responsibility lay with me, with my lack of self-restraint...

Upon my graduation from the academy last year, I started seriously preparing to inherit the family name and title. I followed my father around, assisting him in his work. At my current pace, I would have no issues taking over father's duties. To that end, however, I had to soon find a fiancée of my own.

I was already eighteen. Regardless of my relatively young age, there were calls for me to quickly decide on a fiancée. Perhaps I should have been grateful that there were many noble ladies who were willing to take my hand.

Amongst them, there were quite a few who met all the conditions required by my family. I had even met with some of these women in person. I kept it all a secret from Sophia, of course. She would have many opinions if informed about my activities.

Honestly speaking, however, I would always compare these noble ladies I met... with Katarina. If it were Katarina, she would do this. Or perhaps she would do that — those were the first thoughts that would enter my mind.

No matter the noble lady I met, thoughts of Katarina would surface from the depths of my mind. I could not bring myself to meet with them after that. Thankfully, my parents seemed to have noticed that I had certain complicated feelings toward marriage. While they never rushed me or made any demands of me, I understood that this could not possibly go on.

That was why I made up my mind to finally cut loose these emotions I had harbored for so many years. As such, if Katarina and Jeord left on a journey, and grew closer during it... I would finally be able to bury these emotions for good. Or so I thought.

I had come to the academy to deliver some completed work I had done for the council, but found myself visiting Sophia. She had been very down since Katarina's sudden departure. In fact, Sophia was pacing around rapidly in odd circles.

"I understand you being lonely due to Katarina's journey. However, Katarina is Jeord's fiancé. Is their bond deepening not a good thing?" I said.

"Come now, Big Brother, you're worried as well, aren't you? You're only putting up a brave front... you should really be more honest with yourself!" my sister replied, somewhat rebelliously.

"What are you talking about, Sophia?" I replied, attempting to sound natural. I was shaken within, however, at the fact that my feelings were so easily revealed.

Logically, I would like for Katarina's relationship with Jeord to deepen — so that I may give up and let go. Emotionally, however, it was not the same. I wanted to shout, from the bottom of my heart, that I did not want them to go any further than they already had.

As my logical conclusions and complicated feelings continued layering themselves in my mind, I attempted to keep up with my sister in conversation — the very same sister who, at some point, had learned to speak her mind. It was then that a member of the council appeared; Mary Hunt, a letter in her hands.

Written within, in Katarina's characteristic handwriting, were records of her enjoying the sights and sounds of her journey. From the general tone of her descriptions, it did not seem that her relationship with Jeord had deepened in any meaningful way.

I found myself relieved at this development... which only served to further complicate my churning emotions.

~The Exertions of Raphael Wolt~

I tidied up the various documents I'd been checking and placed them on my desk, then sighed. With this, my work was finally all done.

All I had to do was look up, however, and I would be greeted with a mountain of work — work that never seemed to really be done. *Ugh...* I let another huge sigh escape from my lips, without even realizing it.

This was a room in the Magical Ministry in the department I belonged to. Under normal circumstances, my department always did have more work than others — but the workload I faced now was simply incomparable. This was because my superior, and the most senior individual in this department, was absent.

The reason why our department got so much work in the first place was because this person was terribly impressive. My superior, Larna Smith. From her demeanor and appearance, it would seem that she was a noble — but I did not know much other than that. Her intense curiosity about magecraft and her well-known capabilities saw her propelled to the top echelons of the Ministry, eventually even becoming an executive of sorts. In short, my superior was very good at what she did, but was a little bit of an eccentric.

In fact, she was the first one to suggest that the Ministry take me in, despite the amount of trouble I had caused them. Those around her thought of her as different, maybe even a little bizarre. A while after I had been transferred into her department, I decided to ask Larna why she would have taken in a previous Wielder of Darkness like myself.

At the time, her answer was simple — *"Because you seem interesting."* The moment I heard that, I could not help but agree with her colleagues — Larna Smith was indeed strange.

After I had worked under her for some time, my assumptions were proven correct, time and time again. Larna was a woman who was faithful to her own interests, first and foremost. She simply had to do everything with her own hands, or she wouldn't truly feel at peace. For instance, Larna would often take part in infiltration and investigative missions — excursions that were usually handled by staff below her station. If anyone were to try to stop her, she would set off on her own without a sound either way.

To make things even worse, Larna was an undisputed professional in the art of disguise, to the point where one would wonder how what she did was even possible. Because she would often end up looking like someone else altogether, no one would notice if she decided to act on her own. While she did have set appearances that she used for most of her disguises, even I could not keep track of how she really looked — perhaps she was even disguised on a daily basis.

As a result, Larna basically did whatever she pleased, and was quite a difficult person to work for indeed, especially if she were one's direct superior. While we did have a fair number of complaints to make about Larna as her subordinates, we all did respect her, and I was no exception.

She was reckless in many ways, and would often disappear if you took your eyes off of her for a second. We did a lot of extra work because of her tendencies, but Larna was sure to protect us if anything went wrong. She would always take responsibility for her actions, never blaming her subordinates.

Her knowledge of magecraft was something else as well — along with her sheer ingenuity when it came to inventing magical tools and the like. While we all did complain about Larna Smith, we all respected her in our own ways.

Even so... in a situation such as this one, we were giving it our all, when—

THUD!

I turned my eyes toward the source of the sound — one of my departmental colleagues had fallen, face first, on his table. He most likely lost consciousness from the sheer amount of work we had to go through.

That was to be expected. Even I had been working non-stop these past few days, without a wink of sleep. My superior, Larna, had taken a few of our new staff members out into the field. To give them a good experience, she said... even during such a busy time in the Ministry. This incident stood out for many reasons, of course, earning us the ire of other departments, who did their best to offload as much work onto us as possible.

If Larna had been present, she would have grabbed the proverbial bull by the horns, telling the Ministry that certain tasks simply could not be done. Either that, or she would sit down and simply finish a good half of it on her own. But now, the unfinished work remained stacked like small hills.

Larna's real reason for going out into the field was to investigate the sudden disappearance of Keith Claes, son of Duke Claes. Needless to say, work had to be done with regard to that, too. As a result, our departmental office had been hell on earth for the last few days.

I had worked with Keith together in the student council when I was attending the academy, and it was likely that Dark Magic had been involved in his disappearance. I was certainly worried, so I wanted to do what I could to be useful. The enemy, however, was quite clever themselves, and I simply could not get my hands on any kind of useful information.

On top of that... there was this ever-growing pile of work before me. I could feel my heart slowly breaking. But I could not give in now — I would *not* give up now. As Larna had entrusted everything to me for these past few days, I had no choice but to overcome these obstacles.

To begin with, the fact that Larna had left her work and assignments to some unknown individual who had just been with the Ministry for a little over a year was surprising — not only to me, but to a great number of her colleagues. Perhaps that was why I had to ensure that I executed what I was tasked with to the best of my ability.

I felt deeply for my colleague who had collapsed at his desk, of course... but I would soon have to wake him, by force, if necessary. We could not afford to lose even a single person right now.

Alright then... Just as I gritted my teeth and honed my resolve, mentally preparing myself to dive into yet another mountain of work... there was a knock on our department's door. *Who could it be, at this busy time...?* I felt myself becoming somewhat annoyed.

"Please, do come in," I said, and a familiar face appeared. It was ex-student council member and my colleague, Nicol Ascart. Behind him was a female staff member — she had guided him here, perhaps. Her face was entirely red from blushing. I could see that my friend's alluring aura had not changed in the slightest.

At the very least, this wasn't a visit from some troublesome higher-up from another department, and that was a good thing.

"I was here on business, and thought I would pay you a visit. I see it has become... quite an incident. Are you alright, Raphael?" Nicol's expression clouded slightly as he gazed upon the horror that was our departmental office.

"Quite an incident indeed, yes. I can feel my heart breaking, actually! And so... while I do thank you for visiting me all the way here, I don't really have time for guests. Apologies."

At my words, Nicol withdrew what appeared to be a letter from his pocket. "It would do you well to read this, then. Perhaps it might even mend your almost-broken heart."

Saying so, Nicol handed the letter to me — and written on it were the words of someone I knew very well. I reflexively took it and skimmed over its contents. Written within were carefree and happy descriptions of a certain journey.

She still did not know that her brother had been kidnapped. I suppose she would feel horrible if she knew... but for now, she was still enjoying her journey away from Sorcié. From her wording and tone, I could almost picture her enjoyment — and as Nicol said, I felt my fractured psyche slowly start to recover.

"Thank you. I do feel a little better than before."

"I see," Nicol said, smiling faintly as he retrieved the letter. I could see the female staff member behind him swooning.

Immediately after, a female staff member in my department, who had up until moments ago been deeply engrossed in her work, happened to see Nicol's smile. It was as if she had lost all remnants of her free will. Soon, she was like the woman at the door.

This was bad… yet another one of my colleagues had fallen. *What a disaster…!* Now that it had come to this, I would have him take responsibility for his actions. "Nicol. Do you have any appointments for the rest of the day?"

"Hmm. Not quite, at least until the late afternoon today…"

"Well then, I suppose I'll have you take responsibility for what you did, yes? Quickly now, help me with these tasks! But make sure you don't show anyone that alluring smile of yours!"

"Responsibility…? Alluring smile…?" Nicol seemed confused. Even so, he quickly agreed to help me, perhaps spurred on by my desperate expression.

As expected of Nicol — although he only assisted me for a few hours, quite a lot of work was done. *Perhaps I should ask him for help again next time… if I did that, though, I might as well write off the female staff members in my department for that entire duration. A conundrum, indeed…*

"What are you doing, Katarina?" Jeord asked.

I showed what I was holding in my hands to him. "I thought I'd send a letter."

"A letter, hm?"

"Yes, to tell everyone back at the academy how our trip is going!"

"But Katarina, we are only two days into our journey. In fact, there has not been much in the way of progress, no?" Jeord seemed exasperated.

I felt somewhat embarrassed. He was right, but... "But... but... This is my first trip! I've always wanted to write letters back home while on a trip, you know?" I said, sulking slightly as I did so.

Jeord smiled, though he looked somewhat troubled. "Hmm. I suppose they will really be suffering now, yes. Perhaps a letter would do them some good."

"Hm?"

"Well then, Katarina. I will accompany you — should we have this letter sent?"

"Yes, let's."

And so Jeord and I set off to post the letter back to the academy. On the way there we stopped by a sweets shop, where everything looked delicious! I ended up sharing half of a sweet with Jeord. It was incredibly tasty. I thought I would describe this snack in my letter, too, and how we shared it together.

"It would be best for you to exclude anything of the sort, Katarina," Jeord said, stopping me before I could write down any of it.

I didn't know what that was all about. Jeord just immediately offered to buy me another treat though, so I soon forgot about it.

After we were done eating, we arrived at the post office, and the letter was soon safely on its way.

My Next Life as a VILLAINESS: ALL ROUTES LEAD TO DOOM!

ANNE'S ROOM

TODAY, WE WOULD LIKE TO ASK EVERYONE A QUESTION.

LADY KATARINA'S PERSONAL MAID.

HELLO. I AM ANNE SHELLY,

YOU ARE SUDDENLY EXILED FROM THE KINGDOM! IF YOU COULD BRING ONE THING WITH YOU, WHAT WOULD IT BE?

TO FULLY REALIZE ONE'S POTENTIAL, A FAMILIAR AND FAVORITE TOOL IS ESSENTIAL!

FOR WHEN I'M EMPLOYED AS A FARMER, NATURALLY!

HA!

MY TRUSTY HOE!

KATARINA CLAES

ONE CAN ACHIEVE VERY MUCH.

AS LONG AS ONE HAS A WEAPON OF SOME KIND,

VERY MUCH INDEED.

AH, THAT WOULD BE MY SWORD.

JEORD STUART

I NEED TO HAVE THEM WITH ME TO KEEP HER HAPPY.

MY BIG SISTER DOES GET HUNGRY VERY QUICKLY, AND COMPLAINS QUITE A LOT WHEN SHE DOES. I CARRY A SUPPLY AT ALL TIMES.

HMM... SNACKS, PERHAPS?

KEITH CLAES

THE PIANO'S NICE TOO. NOT THAT I CAN JUST BRING THE THING WITH ME...

BEEN USING IT FOR A WHILE. MY FAVORITE AND ALL.

HUH? MY FAVORITE VIOLIN, I GUESS?

ALAN STUART

COMMON SENSE INDICATES THAT ONE WOULD BE UNABLE TO ACHIEVE ANYTHING WITHOUT APPROPRIATE FUNDING.

FUU

MONETARY RESOURCES.

NICOL ASCART

I COULD NEVER LEAVE THEM BEHIND!

OH... I WOULD TAKE MY FAVORITE BOOKS!

SOPHIA ASCART

EVEN IF I WERE TO GO TO A FOREIGN LAND, THIS WOULD SURELY COME IN USEFUL... IN MANY WAYS.

PERHAPS MY PERSONAL NOTEBOOK? WITH VARIOUS PIECES OF USEFUL INFORMATION ON CERTAIN NOBLES.

EHEHE-HEH...

MARY HUNT

THEY ARE FULL OF MANY WONDERFUL MEMORIES!

I'VE BEEN USING THEM SINCE CHILDHOOD!

WHY, MY BAKING TOOLS, OF COURSE!

MARIA CAMPBELL

AT LEAST PAY ME A FAIR PRICE FOR THE AMOUNT OF WORK I DO...

DUE TO MY SUPERIOR'S ECCENTRICITY, MY WORK-LOAD IS TREMEN-DOUS...

MY... SEVERANCE PAY FROM THE MINISTRY, I SUPPOSE...

RAPHAEL WOLT

AS LONG AS I HAVE THIS BODY OF MINE, I'LL WORK SOMETHING OUT.

NOTHING, REALLY.

SORA

DO YOU MEAN YOU'LL TAKE KATARINA WITH YOU, ANNE...?!

THAT'S ALL FOR TODAY'S PROGRAM...

I AM CONTENT TO SIMPLY BE BY LADY KATARINA'S SIDE.

ANNE'S

HM? AS FOR MYSELF?

THANK YOU FOR YOUR ANSWERS, EVERYONE...

Hello, everyone. This is Satoru Yamaguchi.

It is now the fourth volume of *My Next Life as a Villainess: All Routes Lead to Doom!* I had never imagined that I would end up publishing the fourth volume.

This is all thanks to everyone's support. Thank you very much.

This volume is about a new problem that the protagonist, Katarina, faces as she moves closer to graduation. Her brother Keith runs away from home. Katarina, who assumes that she is responsible for this, ends up gathering the strongest party and leaving on a journey. This volume also features the debut of a cute (?) mascot. I would be very happy if you enjoy reading it.

I would also like to once again thank Nami Hidaka-sama, who provided the illustrations for this volume, and all the previous volumes. The omake manga was wonderful as well. Thank you very much.

Lastly, I would like to thank the editorial department and publishing staff, as well as any and all who have lent me their kind assistance during the publishing process. I thank you from the bottom of my heart.

Everyone, thank you very much.

Satoru Yamaguchi

2

VOLUME 2
ON SALE NOW!

Author: **Ameko Kaeruda**
Illustrator: **Kazutomo Miy**

SEXILED

My Sexist Party Leader Kicked Me Out,
So I Teamed Up With a Mythical Sorceres

MANGA VOLUME 2
ON SALE NOW!

ASCENDANCE
OF A
BOOKWORM
I'll do anything to
become a librarian!

Part 1 If there aren't any
books, I'll just have
to make some! II

Author: Miya Kazuki / Artist: Suzuka
Character Designer: You Shiina

ASCENDANCE
OF A
BOOKWORM

I'll do anything to
become a librarian

Part 2 Apprentice Shrine
Maiden Vol. 3

Author: **Miya Kazuki**
Illustrator: **You Shiina**

NOVEL:
PART 2 VOL. 3
ON SALE NOW!

04

ASO HANAMURA

ANIMETA!

VOLUME 4
ON SALE NOW!

Author
FUNA

Illust.
SUKIMA

3

VOLUME 3
ON SALE
DECEMBER 2020!

MANGA VOLUME 2
ON SALE
JANUARY 2021!

I SHALL SURVIVE USING POTIONS!

HEY /////////
▶ **HAVE YOU HEARD OF**
J-Novel Club?

It's the digital publishing company that brings you the latest novels from Japan!

Subscribe today at

▶▶▶ **j-novel.club** ◀◀◀

and read the latest volumes as they're translated, or become a premium member to get a *FREE* ebook every month!

Check Out The Latest Volume Of
**MY NEXT LIFE AS A VILLAINESS:
ALL ROUTES LEAD TO DOOM!**

Plus the rest of our J-Novel Heart and Club Titles Including:

▶ The Tales of Marielle Clarac
▶ Bibliophile Princess
▶ Can Someone Please Explain What's Going On?!
▶ The Epic Tale of the Reincarnated Prince Herscherik

...and many more!

▶ The Extraordinary, the Ordinary, and SOAP!
▶ Deathbound Duke's Daughter
▶ I Refuse to Be Your Enemy!
▶ Ascendance of a Bookworm
▶ Sexiled: My Sexist Party Leader Kicked Me Out, So I Teamed Up With a Mythical Sorceress!

In Another World With My Smartphone, Illustration © Eiji Usatsuka   *Arifureta: From Commonplace to World's Strongest*, Illustration © Takayaki

J-Novel Club Lineup

Ebook Releases Series List

A Lily Blooms in Another World
A Wild Last Boss Appeared!
Altina the Sword Princess
Amagi Brilliant Park
An Archdemon's Dilemma:
    How to Love Your Elf Bride
Arifureta Zero
Arifureta: From Commonplace
    to World's Strongest
Ascendance of a Bookworm
Beatless
Bibliophile Princess
Black Summoner
By the Grace of the Gods
Campfire Cooking in Another
    World with My Absurd Skill
Can Someone Please Explain
    What's Going On?!
Cooking with Wild Game
Crest of the Stars
Deathbound Duke's Daughter
Demon Lord, Retry!
Der Werwolf: The Annals of Veight
From Truant to Anime Screenwriter:
    My Path to "Anohana" and "The
    Anthem of the Heart"
Full Metal Panic!
Grimgar of Fantasy and Ash
Her Majesty's Swarm
Holmes of Kyoto
How a Realist Hero Rebuilt the
    Kingdom
How NOT to Summon a Demon
    Lord
I Refuse to Be Your Enemy!
I Saved Too Many Girls and Caused
    the Apocalypse
I Shall Survive Using Potions!
In Another World With My
    Smartphone
Infinite Dendrogram
Infinite Stratos
Invaders of the Rokujouma!?
Isekai Rebuilding Project
JK Haru is a Sex Worker in Another
    World
Kobold King
Kokoro Connect
Last and First Idol
Lazy Dungeon Master
Mapping: The Trash-Tier Skill That
    Got Me Into a Top-Tier Party

Middle-Aged Businessman, Arise in
    Another World!
Mixed Bathing in Another
    Dimension
Monster Tamer
My Big Sister Lives in a Fantasy
    World
My Instant Death Ability is So
    Overpowered, No One in This
    Other World Stands a Chance
    Against Me!
My Next Life as a Villainess: All
    Routes Lead to Doom!
Otherside Picnic
Outbreak Company
Outer Ragna
Record of Wortenia War
Seirei Gensouki: Spirit Chronicles
Sexiled: My Sexist Party Leader
    Kicked Me Out, So I Teamed Up
    With a Mythical Sorceress!
Slayers
Sorcerous Stabber Orphen:
    The Wayward Journey
Tearmoon Empire
Teogonia
The Bloodline
The Combat Butler and Automaton
    Waitress
The Economics of Prophecy
The Epic Tale of the Reincarnated
    Prince Herscherik
The Extraordinary, the Ordinary,
    and SOAP!
The Greatest Magicmaster's
    Retirement Plan
The Holy Knight's Dark Road
The Magic in this Other World is
    Too Far Behind!
The Master of Ragnarok & Blesser
    of Einherjar
The Sorcerer's Receptionist
The Tales of Marielle Clarac
The Underdog of the Eight Greater
    Tribes
The Unwanted Undead Adventurer
WATARU!! The Hot-Blooded
    Fighting Teen & His Epic
    Adventures in a Fantasy World
    After Stopping a Truck with His
    Bare Hands!!

The White Cat's Revenge as
    Plotted from the Demon King's
    Lap
The World's Least Interesting
    Master Swordsman
Welcome to Japan, Ms. Elf!
When the Clock Strikes Z
Wild Times with a Fake Fake
    Princess

Manga Series:

A Very Fairy Apartment
An Archdemon's Dilemma:
    How to Love Your Elf Bride
Animeta!
Ascendance of a Bookworm
Bibliophile Princess
Black Summoner
Campfire Cooking in Another
    World with My Absurd Skill
Cooking with Wild Game
Demon Lord, Retry!
Discommunication
How a Realist Hero Rebuilt the
    Kingdom
I Love Yuri and I Got Bodyswapped
    with a Fujoshi!
I Shall Survive Using Potions!
Infinite Dendrogram
Mapping: The Trash-Tier Skill That
    Got Me Into a Top-Tier Party
Marginal Operation
Record of Wortenia War
Seirei Gensouki: Spirit Chronicles
Sorcerous Stabber Orphen:
    The Reckless Journey
Sorcerous Stabber Orphen:
    The Youthful Journey
Sweet Reincarnation
The Faraway Paladin
The Magic in this Other World is
    Too Far Behind!
The Master of Ragnarok & Blesser
    of Einherjar
The Tales of Marielle Clarac
The Unwanted Undead Adventurer

Keep an eye out at j-novel.club
for further new title
announcements!